NEIL YOUNG

Other titles in the series

The Clash
Leonard Cohen
Elvis Costello
Tom Waits

NEIL YOUNG

Alexis Petridis

Published by Unanimous Ltd
254–258 Goswell Road, London EC1V 7RL

A CIP catalogue record for this book is
available from the British Library.

Series Editor: John Aizlewood
Project Editor: Nicola Birtwisle

ISBN: 1 903318 00 9

Printed in Italy

1 2 3 4 5 6 7 8 9

Acknowledgments
Thanks to John Aizlewood and Simon Majumdar for their extreme patience above
and beyond the call of duty. I'm thankful to Josh Blackburn for his country home
and to Andy Pemberton for his advice and support. There are a host of excellent
Neil Young-related websites on the net. For a remarkable alternative view of Young's
career, his father Scott Young's *Neil and Me* comes highly recommended, as does
anything Crosby, Stills, Nash and Young-related with Johnny Rogan's name on it.

CONTENTS

ONE

THE STORY

Neil Young has never been the most forthcoming of rock legends. During the early 1970s, he avoided the press almost entirely. Incredulous journalists were informed that the singer-songwriter with the lyrics about racism, ecology, drugs and death had nothing to say, while more recently he has used the superstar's prerogative to deflect questions: 'I just don't want to talk about that.' He has been particularly reticent about his childhood. 'I had a pretty good upbringing,' he told one interviewer, after a lengthy and foreboding silence. 'I remember really good things about both my parents...I think back on my childhood and I remember moving around a lot, from school to school.'

But if Young's interviews have been deliberately vague about his early years, his songs have been perversely frank. Neil Percival Ragland Young was born in Toronto on November 12, 1945, the second son of middle-class parents: his father Scott was a sports journalist and short-story writer, his mother Edna, always known by her childhood nickname of Rassy, later found fame as a panellist on the long-running Canadian quiz show Twenty Questions. In August 1948, when Scott Young decided to write fiction full-time, he moved the family to Omemee, the town in north Ontario his son later detailed in 'Helpless', his exquisite contribution to Crosby, Stills Nash & Young's multi-platinum 1971 album *Déjà Vu*.

A potentially fatal brush with Canada's 1951 polio epidemic aside, Young's early childhood was pastoral and uneventful. His father's affair with a woman he met on an assignment for *Sports Illustrated* in 1954, however, precipitated a series of separations, reunions and upheavals that would continue until the Youngs finally divorced six years later. The family moved from Omemee back to Toronto, home of rock radio station 1050-CHUM.

'That's when I really became aware of what was going on in music,' Young told Rolling Stone in the late 1970s. 'I knew then that I wanted to play, that I was into it. Maybe The Chantels, Short Fat Fannie, Elvis Presley, Larry Williams, Chuck Berry, those were the first people I heard. I used to fall asleep listening to music. I was a real swinger those weekends: I'd stay up late listening to the radio.'

Young persuaded his father to buy him a plastic ukulele in Christmas 1958, which he quickly upgraded to a cheap acoustic guitar. His nascent musical considerations were over-shadowed by another of his father's extramarital affairs, with a public relations worker called Astrid Mead, who would become Scott Young's second wife. This time, the separation was final: Scott left home, while Rassy moved Neil and his older brother Bob (born 1942) to Winnipeg, an event depicted in Young's 1973 epic 'Don't Be Denied'.

Young was easy prey to the class bullies: a gangling, sickly child from out of town, academically indifferent, with a nervous penchant for biting his fingernails. But Kelvin High School also introduced him to other kids his age who were equally stirred by 1050-CHUM's crackling diet of Chuck Berry and Shadows records. Classmate Ken Koblun played bass guitar. With Rassy Young's vociferous encouragement and an endless stream of other young Winnipeg musicians filling in, the pair formed The

Jades, then Stardust, then The Esquires, who came complete with their own business card: 'The Esquires. Instrumental and Vocal Styling. Fine Music and Entertainment.'

Young took charge of the band, hiring and firing musicians and writing instrumentals in the style of The Shadows: 'Banana Mashed', 'Panic Button', 'Comanche'. With their name shortened to The Squires, the band began to pick up a local following on the teen dance circuit. On one occasion, a school official fearful of rowdy fans attempted to cancel a Squires concert, only to suffer the wrath of Young's mother, formidable in a crisis. 'I told the idiot that if he wanted to cancel the dance that was fine with me,' Rassy later explained. 'The contract read that The Squires got paid regardless. He soon backed down.'

In 1963, The Squires even made a single for local label V Records, coupling two Young instrumentals, 'The Sultan' and 'Image In Blue'. By then, however, Hank Marvin had been supplanted in Young's affections by The Beatles. He began introducing vocal numbers into The Squires' sets in January 1964. An unsure version of 'Money (That's What I Want)' marked the first appearance of Young's distinctive voice, high-pitched, wavering, occasionally off-key. Its effect on the audience was instantaneous. 'Stick to instrumentals!' screamed one disgruntled fan. At a recording session later that year, the producer told Young he would never make it as a singer. 'I just kept at it,' remembered Young. 'My voice is a little strange.'

In September 1964, Young quit school for a full-time musical career. The Squires drove to Fort William in Young's 1948 Buick hearse, nicknamed Mort, to play the Flamingo Club Tavern. By now billed as Rock 'n' Rolling Neil Young & The Squires, the band's sound was original to the point of being slightly bizarre. After being exposed to folk (and a young Joni Mitchell) at Winnipeg's Fourth Dimension coffee house, Young had begun writing his own acoustic material and penned perennial live favourite 'Sugar Mountain' on his nineteenth birthday in his Fort William hotel room. The Squires, meanwhile, took traditional folk songs and played them on electric instruments.

'It was different from anything else I did before or after,' he said. 'It was minor key, folk, punk, rock kind of thing. We did 'Clementine' and 'She'll Be Coming Round The Mountain'. We changed them totally with rock 'n' roll arrangements.'

On 18 April 1965, another touring band, a five-piece New York folk outfit called The Company, arrived at Fort William's Fourth Dimension to see The Squires hammering out 'Cotton Fields' and 'Tom Dooley' in a garage-punk style. Intrigued and impressed, their guitarist Stephen Stills introduced himself to Young at the end of the set.

'Neil was playing folk-rock before anybody else,' said Stills, a bored veteran of several folk bands, including the mild-mannered Au Go Go Singers, who had cut a 1964 album for the Mafia-run label Roulette. 'We had a great time, running about in his hearse, drinking good, strong Canadian beer and being young. At first I thought, "Well, I'm gonna quit this idiot group and go play with him right now."'

Young was impressed with Stills's raw, soulful voice, Ken Koblun fell for Company vocalist Jean Gurney, and a bond between the two bands was cemented. Stills, now more interested in The Beatles than acoustic renditions of 'Froggy Went A-Courtin'', gave Young his Greenwich Village address and told him to look him up if he came to New York. The Squires and The Company went their separate ways: the full significance of their meeting would not become apparent for several years.

Next, The Squires tried their luck in the big city, Toronto. It was an ill-fated trip. Mort finally gave up the ghost, leaving the band stranded in Blind River, an incident documented eleven years later in Young's song 'Long May You Run', the title track to The Stills-Young Band's only album. The Squires attempted to hitch-hike separately to Toronto, but one of Young's rides beat him up, throwing him into a ditch with a cry of 'hippie!'.

On arrival in Toronto, The Squires found themselves in penury. Young had to appeal to his father for a $400 loan. By the end of the summer, they had broken up. Ken Koblun played bass in various bands around Yorkville, Toronto's own miniature Greenwich Village, while Young moved in with a folk singer, Vicky Taylor, and attempted to launch a solo career. It was an unmitigated disaster. 'There was a review of one of my shows in a newspaper and it said all my songs were like a cliché,' he remembered. 'Toronto was a very humbling experience for me.'

Young's misery and poverty inspired a string of songs that depicted himself as a moody, troubled outsider, an image that would serve him well in the early years of his recording career. 'Nowadays Clancy Can't Even Sing' told the story of a Winnipeg schoolfriend ostracised for his peculiar habit of singing 'The Happy Wanderer' between lessons. 'Don't Pity Me Babe' resurfaced on Young's 1975 album *Zuma*, re-titled 'Don't Cry No Tears'. In 1965, however, no one was interested.

Young, reduced to working in a bookstore stock room (after the obligatory haircut), decided to tag along when Koblun visited Jean Gurney in New York, hoping to bump into Stephen Stills. But Stills had already tried to contact Young in Toronto, discovered he was 'living with this folk singer chick who'd convinced him he was Bob Dylan' and had left for California and an audition as a songwriter for The Monkees, 'in disgust' at Young's decision to abandon rock for folk. The only other musician to be found at Gurney's apartment was Richie Furay, who had sung with Stills in the Au Go Go Singers. It was better than nothing: Young taught the impressed, youthful vocalist 'Nowadays Clancy Can't Even Sing', but returned to Toronto, dismayed, after three days. A second visit to New York some months later yielded a demo session for Elektra ('Nowadays Clancy Can't Even Sing', 'Sugar Mountain' and 'Don't Pity Me Babe' were among the songs recorded), but no record deal.

Young returned to the unwelcoming coffee houses of Yorkville, and his stillborn career as a folk singer. Shortly after his return, he met Bruce Palmer, a bass player who had achieved a minor level of notoriety as a member of Jack London & The Sparrows, a band fronted by an English expat who fuelled the omnipresent Beatlemania by talking onstage in a Liverpool accent, helpfully ignoring the fact that his family had emigrated to Canada in 1948. London's cover was finally blown when he announced a song in thick Scouse, then turned to his band and audibly berated them in his natural Canadian voice. 'The crowd started booing and throwing things,' remembered one onlooker.

Dumping their lead singer, the other Sparrows went on to join Steppenwolf, but Palmer was now working with The Mynah Birds, a similarly gimmicky act named after a local club, who performed with a live mynah bird flapping around their heads. They did, however, have a secret weapon, an American lead singer, born James Johnson, but now called Ricky James Matthews, who had a local reputation as 'the black Mick Jagger' and a combustible national career to come when he ditched his surname and became Rick James.

The band's lead guitarist had recently quit, and Palmer offered Young the post. Despite the fact that he no longer owned an electric guitar – he had traded his for a 12-string acoustic – Young accepted. 'I had to eat,' he recalled, 'this was the first time I was in a group where I wasn't calling the shots.' He balanced the loss of control against a more compelling point: The Mynah Birds were bankrolled by local millionaire entrepreneur John Craig Eaton.

Eaton's partner Morley Shuman mysteriously arranged a deal with Motown, a first for a predominantly white band. A couple of weeks after joining The Mynah Birds, Young found himself in Detroit, playing his 12-string at an album session produced by Smokey Robinson.

'These guys – Berry Gordy or one of the other heavies,

Holland-Dozier-Holland – would come in,' Young remembered in 1982. 'If we needed something, or they thought we weren't strong enough, a couple of Motown singers would just walk right in and they'd sing the part. If someone wasn't confident or didn't have it, they didn't say "Let's work on this". Some guy would come in who had it. And all of a sudden it was Motown. That's why all those records sounded like that.'

However, the sessions, and The Mynah Birds' fledgling career, were about to end, simultaneously and dramatically. It emerged that the future Rick James had gone AWOL from the US Navy. He was arrested in the studio and imprisoned. Motown immediately cancelled the session and the band's contract.

Returning to Toronto, once again penniless and effectively without a band, Young and Palmer decided to try their luck in Los Angeles, where Young knew Stephen Stills was now residing. They sold the instruments John Eaton had bought on credit and Young bought another hearse for the journey, a 1953 Pontiac. Several friends came along for the ride, the group electing to cross into the USA at the quiet Ontario border town of Sault Ste. Marie, lest their illegal immigrant status and copious supply of marijuana be discovered.

With no money for overnight hotel stops and with Young concerned about the aged hearse breaking down – 'I didn't want another Blind River' – the singer insisted on driving day and night. Eventually, he collapsed from exhaustion in Albuquerque, New Mexico. The others elected to stay there, so after a couple of days convalescence, Young and Palmer continued the journey unaccompanied.

On arrival in Los Angeles, Stills was nowhere to be found among the Sunset Strip clubs and musicians' hang-outs. Young and Palmer had no contacts, no money and nowhere to stay. They survived for a few days by chauffeuring unwitting hipsters in the hearse, before deciding to head north to San Francisco.

What happened next is rock folklore at its most cinematic. Certainly Young and Palmer were driving on Sunset Boulevard.

According to whose version of the story you choose to believe, Stephen Stills and Richie Furay were either walking past, driving on the other side of the road or stuck behind them in a traffic jam. Noticing the hearse's Canadian plates and remembering Mort from Fort William, Stills ran over to discover Young and Palmer.

The quartet reconvened later that day, to smoke grass and play. Stills and Furay startled Young with their dramatic arrangement of 'Nowadays Clancy Can't Even Sing', remembered by Furay from Young's 1965 trip to New York. Barry Friedman, a rock entrepreneur who had befriended Stills and become his manager, put the four in a house on Fountain Street and recommended them to Jim Dickson and Ed Tickner, managers of The Byrds, who in turn lent them equipment and suggested Canadian Dewey Martin, formerly in the employ of country star Faron Young, as a drummer. He agreed to join the new band if he were allowed to sing Wilson Pickett's 'In The Midnight Hour' as part of their set.

The new quintet named themselves Buffalo Springfield, after a steamroller company who were resurfacing Fountain Street during an early rehearsal. They were almost overburdened with talent: three singer-songwriters (Young, Stills, Furay); two lead guitarists (Young, Stills), a drummer who could sing, a bass player who left musicians such as The Byrds' Chris Hillman awestruck, and a potential heart-throb in Furay, who had developed a cute gimmick of tiptoeing across the stage with his feet turned inwards that made teen girls dissolve.

This surfeit of ability would quickly prove the band's undoing, but initially, it simply meant they progressed with dizzying speed and much mutual admiration. After only a week of rehearsals at the seedy Hollywood Center Motel, Buffalo Springfield played their first gig – all original material, save 'In The Midnight Hour' – on April 15, 1966, supporting The Byrds at San Bernardino's Swing Auditorium.

Five more support gigs followed, before their friendship with

Chris Hillman secured them a residency at Sunset Strip's premier club, the Whisky-A-Go-Go, where Buffalo Springfield were residents there for six weeks, playing alongside regulars PF Sloan's Grass Roots and Love. They were an immediate success, attracting the attention not only of fellow musicians such as The Mamas & The Papas, The Byrds and The Hollies, but also of teen magazines *Tigerbeat* and *TeenSet*. The latter were attracted by the group's individual onstage personas: while Furay played up to the girls and Stills sported a cowboy hat to cover his thinning hair, Young's fringed jackets, Comanche war shirts and glowering cool had him marked as the band's 'Hollywood Indian'.

The former members of Buffalo Springfield agree that their Whisky residency represented the band's musical peak – 'the Whisky was as good as we ever were, as dynamic as we ever were, as close as we ever were,' Furay recalled fondly – but it was also the first time that friction between the band's three potential frontmen emerged. 'Neil flipped out at the Whisky and so did I and so did Bruce,' admitted Stills, 'because immediately there were all these chicks hanging out and feeding us more and better dope.'

Other clouds appeared on the horizon during the Whisky residency. They ditched manager Friedman in favour of Charlie Greene and Brian Stone, former representatives of Sonny & Cher, who sold themselves as managers, producers and publishers rolled into one. Although Young would later refer to the duo as 'weasels in the woodwork', in mid-1966 the nascent Buffalo Springfield were dazzled by their stretch limousine, offers of new equipment and accounts at clothing stores and, inevitably, a plentiful supply of drugs.

Young, meanwhile, had begun suffering epileptic seizures, which would plague him throughout Buffalo Springfield. The first occurred while he and Palmer were in a Los Angeles department store. Soon, they would be happening onstage with an alarming frequency.

By July, Greene and Stone had secured a support slot at The Rolling Stones' Hollywood Bowl concert and a $12,000 deal with Atlantic offshoot Atco. But Buffalo Springfield's debut single, a reworking of Young's 'Nowadays Clancy Can't Even Sing', was only a regional hit, while their eponymous debut album suffered from Greene and Stone's clumsy production.

If 'For What It's Worth', Stills's timeless response to the November 12 riot on Sunset Strip, remedied the band's lack of commercial success by reaching Number 7 on the American singles chart, it could do little to paper over the ever-widening cracks in the band itself.

In late 1966, there had been a short-lived plot to replace Dewey Martin with Alexander 'Skip' Spence, later of Moby Grape. Bruce Palmer's gargantuan appetite for LSD led to several drug busts, while Young also fell foul of the law, suffering a beating from police as he was arrested for outstanding parking violations. Matters came to a head during a disastrous attempt at combining a residency at New York club Ondines with some recording sessions in January 1967. The sessions were fraught. 'There were a lot of distractions: groupies, drugs,' remembered Young. 'All the clubs, places to go, things to do. I remember being haunted suddenly by this whole obsession with "How do I fit in here?"'

The gigs were even worse. Stills punched Palmer midway through a set. Young had another epileptic fit onstage. Finally, Palmer was busted in his hotel room and deported back to Canada, where he remained for four months. According to Richie Furay, 'that's when the whole thing fell apart.'

Buffalo Springfield struggled on through more gigs, abortive recording sessions and television appearances with various substitute bassists, including Ken Koblun. Both Young and Stills began recording separately from the rest of the band: Young with producer Jack Nitzsche, Stills with The Byrds' David Crosby. When Palmer snuck back across the border disguised as a businessman and rejoined Buffalo Springfield in May 1967, it seemed as though the band had regained some stability. But a few days later, on the eve of their debut on the Johnny Carson Show and a fortnight before the prestigious Monterey Pop Festival, Young called a meeting to announce he was leaving the band. 'Something inside of me felt like I wasn't quite on the right track,' he later said. He didn't want to be on Carson's show; he was sick both of the circus that surrounded the band (as his increasingly bitter lyrics showed) and of constantly fighting Stills for dominance.

'Part of my upbringing in the south was very militaristic,' admitted Stills. 'I was in this military school and being taught how to be an officer. A lot of the ways I relate to situations like that is to simply take command. Of course, somebody like Neil or Bruce is instantly going to rebel.'

While Young busied himself recording with Jack Nitzsche (who offered a more prosaic interpretation of Young's departure: he wanted 'lots of money and star fame'), Buffalo Springfield struggled on. They were fired one night from a Boston club residency and turned in a desultory performance at Monterey with a clearly unrehearsed David Crosby filling in. Young's replacement, Doug Hastings, failed to fit in, but Young too was having problems. 'I couldn't get Atlantic to let me go,' he explained. 'So it was a choice between not working at all or going back to the group. Finally, I was starving to death. I didn't have any money.' Despite Dewey Martin and Richie Furay's misgivings, Young rejoined on August 10.

It was a fragile truce borne out of necessity. Piecemeal sessions for a second album continued, but the end result, *Buffalo Springfield Again*, released in December 1967, was essentially a collection of solo efforts of varying quality.

'It wasn't the cohesive unit that made the debut album,' admits Furay, who hardly helped matters by contributing a stinging attack on Young called 'A Child's Claim To Fame'. Neither 'Rock 'n' Roll Woman' nor 'Bluebird', both Stills compositions, made much of an impression on the singles chart, and managers Greene and Stone were finally fired. All of the band wanted Elliot Roberts, Joni Mitchell's manager, to handle their affairs, but Young mysteriously refused to sign the contract, telling Roberts to get lost. Instead, road manager Dickie Davis took over.

A November tour with The Beach Boys provided some stability, Young striking up a friendship with hedonistic drummer Dennis Wilson, who even introduced Young to his little friend The Wizard, better known as Charles Manson.

'He was great,' recalled Young of the wannabe pop star who would mastermind the Tate-La Bianca murders. 'He was unreal. He was really, really good. Scary. I actually went to Mo Ostin [then-head of Warner Brothers] and suggested they sign him. I said, "There's this guy, Charlie Manson, he plays these unique songs and he should be on Warner Brothers records." I mean, if he'd had a band like Dylan had had on 'Subterranean Homesick Blues', then… But he was never going to get that band because there was just something about him that stopped anybody being around him for too long. He was too intense. I was always thinking, "What's he going to do next? I'd better get out this guy's way before he explodes." So I did.'

The full horror of Manson's 'intensity' would not become apparent for another eighteen months, but Young had more immediate problems on his mind. The tour with The Beach Boys had proved only a brief respite. The atmosphere within Buffalo Springfield had never been worse. On January 26, 1968, the band played a concert at the UCLA Irvine that, according to Dewey Martin, ended in a backstage fist fight between Young and Stills. Afterwards, Palmer, whose appetite for drugs remained insatiable, was busted twice in the same night. This time, the other members decided to let him go, replacing him with past and future Poco member Jim Messina. In February, Young stopped attending the sporadic recording sessions for the band's third album. He returned a month later.

'I just couldn't handle it towards the end,' he remembered in

1975. 'It wasn't me scheming on a solo career, it wasn't anything but my nerves. Everything started to go too fucking fast. I was going crazy, joining and quitting and joining again. I began to feel like I didn't have to answer or obey anyone. I needed more space, so I'd quit then come back, because it sounded so good.'

The final break came after another drug bust on March 20, 1968. This time only Martin and Stills (who climbed out of a bedroom window) escaped. Eric Clapton, who was jamming with the band, was also arrested. Shortly afterwards, Young turned up unexpectedly at the house of Elliot Roberts, the prospective Springfield manager he had rejected a few months previously. He asked Roberts to manage him as a solo artist. Roberts agreed.

Buffalo Springfield played a farewell gig on May 5 at the Long Beach Sports Arena, in front of a crowd of tearful Los Angeles teenyboppers. Backstage, Young announced to reporters that he was already negotiating a solo deal. The next month, he began work on his eponymous debut album.

Young retreated to Topanga, a mountainous region of Hollywood. He used his advance from new label Reprise to buy a four-storey house, a 'comfortable fucking place', isolated in the hills. The remainder of 1968 was far removed from the chaos of Buffalo Springfield's final months. He worked on his album with Jack Nitzsche and David Briggs, who had offered Young a lift one day in his army surplus personnel carrier and had somehow ended up producing him. Young found his drug charge reduced to one of disturbing the peace. He romanced folk singer Robin Lane, an affair which ended, Young admitted, because 'too often when I got home, I picked up the guitar instead of the girl.' He then struck up a relationship with the proprietor of a Topanga restaurant, Susan Acevado, a divorcee with a seven-year old daughter. Six months later, they impulsively married. It was December 1968.

'I thought that would help, I guess,' explained Young. 'I thought that would ground me out. I was looking to get some kind of stability.'

The domestic stability countered Young's professional insecurities, which had not waned since the Buffalo Springfield days described in *Buffalo Springfield Again*'s 'Mr. Soul'. A series of acoustic gigs with Joni Mitchell at New York's Bottom Line club had been poorly received in October, while the sessions for his album were blighted by the introduction of a new recording process called CSG, designed to make the mono and stereo mixes sound identical. Initially enthusiastic, Young later dismissed CSG as 'new fangled-bullshit...a piece of shit idea' and remixed the record without it. The critical response was lukewarm.

'It took me all the time it took to make those Buffalo Springfield records and almost all my first album to figure out I had to go back to the way I started in Winnipeg, back in Thunder Bay when I was recorded live, in order to get my sound just right,' he told Nick Kent in 1989.

Young had already met the band who would enable him to achieve this goal. While recording the first Buffalo Springfield album, he had become friendly with The Rockets, originally a doo-wop group from New York called Danny & The Memories. Young had initially infiltrated their circle in order to get close to bassist Billy Talbot's girlfriend – Robin Lane – but their leader, Danny Whitten, had won Young over by praising and encouraging his attempts at singing. After a few evenings jamming at The Rockets' Laurel Canyon home, however, the madness of Buffalo Springfield had swallowed up Young and they lost contact. The Rockets had gone on to release an unsuccessful, eponymous album on The Turtles' label, White Whale, in 1968.

In late February 1969, however, Young spotted The Rockets' name outside the Whisky A-Go-Go, and decided to renew his acquaintance, asking if he could sit in with them. The band agreed, and at the end of their residency, asked Whitten, Talbot and Molina if they would join him in a new band, which he first christened War Babies, then changed to Crazy Horse. They agreed, on the condition that they also continued as The Rockets. Young agreed, then imposed a schedule on them that made that arrangement impossible.

After only a week of rehearsal, the quartet recorded 'Cinnamon Girl', 'Cowgirl In The Sand' and 'Down By The River', three songs Young had written in one day while in bed with a fever. They formed the cornerstone of the first Neil Young With Crazy Horse album, *Everybody Knows This Is Nowhere,* released in May 1969 after a series of showcase gigs at the Whisky A-Go-Go. Distorted, instinctive, spontaneous, and thunderously loud, the sound could not have been further from Young's overproduced solo debut. 'Crazy Horse bring out a part of me that's very primitive,' Young observed. 'We really put out a lot of emotion, which is easy for a kid to relate to.'

Among the audience at the Whisky gigs was Stephen Stills. His own post-Springfield project was an acoustic trio in collaboration with The Byrds' David Crosby and former Hollies vocalist Graham Nash, initially called The Frozen Noses in tribute to their copious consumption of cocaine. The name had wisely been altered to Crosby, Stills & Nash. Their self-titled debut album, packed with gentle musical emollients perfectly in tune with the prevalent comedown from flower power, was readied for release, and a tour had been planned. 'David and Graham were in favour of us going out as a sort of augmented Simon & Garfunkel,' explained Stills, 'but I didn't want to. I wanted a band.'

The answer was to find an extra musician to fill out the acoustic sound. Stills approached Steve Winwood and blues organist Mark Naftalin (briefly a member of Janis Joplin's band), only to be turned down, before Atlantic president Ahmet Ertegun suggested Young. After some persuasion – it was, after all, Young who kept leaving and rejoining Buffalo

Springfield whenever the mood took him – Stills agreed.

'Stills came up to my house and asked me to join the group,' says Young. 'I thought about it and said "maybe". Then they weren't sure they wanted to put my name in with theirs. I told them, "no way". So then, after my name was included, I thought, "shit, well, sure I'll do this, but only as long as I can do my own thing with Crazy Horse at the same time." So I did both.'

While choosing to play with both Crosby, Stills, Nash & Young and Crazy Horse led to a punishing schedule throughout the summer of 1969, it was to prove the most astute and fortuitous decision of Young's career. He had ensured himself a role in the musical aggregation that was about to become the biggest group on the planet, while maintaining enough distance to ensure he would never truly be damaged by their drug-inflated egotism.

That Young was different to Crosby, Stills & Nash is illustrated by his attitude to their second gig, the appearance at Woodstock that turned the quartet into superstars. Graham Nash, who had hungrily swallowed the hippie dream as only a man who had spent the mid-1960s singing songs like 'Jennifer Eccles' could, was still evoking Woodstock's 'special magic' five years after the event. Young, by contrast, was utterly unimpressed: 'I thought it was a joke. I wasn't really into it. I didn't even know what I was doing there. I still don't know. I know that I couldn't hardly hear myself when we were playing.'

Young tersely refused to be filmed onstage or even mentioned in the Woodstock film, but with Crosby, Stills, Nash & Young widely acclaimed as the festival's biggest hit, he could do nothing to stem the tide of positive publicity that followed. Their subsequent concerts in 1969 were ecstatically received: they even escaped the horror of Altamont unscathed. Young's solo career was also affected in the wake of Woodstock. *Everybody Knows This Is Nowhere* went platinum, while his debut album was re-promoted with the faintly embarrassing slogan '_____, _____, _____ & Young'.

Advance orders for the quartet's own debut, *Déjà Vu*, were worth a mind-boggling $2,000,000. The painstaking sessions for the album, which eventually lasted six months, were interrupted in the most horrific manner imaginable when Crosby's girlfriend Christine Hinton was killed in a car accident in September: 'David went to identify the body,' observed Nash, disturbingly, 'and he's never been the same since.'

Déjà Vu was released on March 23, 1970 to resounding critical plaudits and became that year's best-selling record in the USA. The tour which followed in May, however, was the clearest demonstration yet that all was not well behind the facade of hippie brotherhood. The bickering between the quartet was endless.

After just one gig in Denver, Crosby, Stills, Nash & Young split up, only to reconvene a week later to record 'Ohio', Young's brilliant, anguished response to the National Guard's killing of four students at Kent State University that same month. They returned to the tour, netting a staggering $50,000 a night for their appearances, but not even such financial rewards could keep the band together. By July, Nash had begun a relationship with singer Rita Coolidge, whom Stills also had romantic designs on. Crosby, Stills, Nash & Young broke up again.

There were more dark clouds brewing over Young's parallel career with Crazy Horse, who, remarkably, had kept gigging and recording throughout the outbreak of Crosby, Stills, Nash & Young mania. It was widely rumoured that all Danny Whitten's love lyrics were inspired by the same 16-year-old girl who had broken his heart. But the failed romance had also sent Whitten's drug use spiralling out of control.

'In those days,' recalled Billy Talbot, 'people just started shooting right up. He just shot some speed, the next day some smack and from then on, he was a junkie.'

Whitten was certainly not the only member of Crazy Horse using hard drugs, but the quantity of heroin he used startled even his fellow band members. 'He was a strong personality and a strong junkie,' said Talbot. 'Did more than anyone else, so they tell me.'

By April 1970, midway through the sessions for Young's third album, *After The Gold Rush*, Whitten's condition had deteriorated to the point that Young decided to fire not just Whitten, but all of Crazy Horse.

The album was completed without them, recorded, for the most part, among the animal skins and candles of Young's Topanga Canyon home. If *After The Gold Rush* was intended to symbolise domestic contentment, however, it came too late. Shortly after the album's release in October 1970, Young's marriage broke down, compounded by the hangers-on who had invaded Topanga Canyon.

'I just had too many fucking people hanging around who didn't know me,' said Young. 'They were parasites whether they intended to be or not. They lived off me, used my money to buy things, used my telephone to make their calls. I didn't like having to be boss and I don't like having to say "get the fuck out."'

After the marriage break-up, Young moved to a ranch in San Mateo county, bought with cash. Shortly after moving in, he slipped a disc lifting heavy slabs of wood while decorating. He would spend the next two years in and out of hospital and traction, restricted to playing acoustic music as he was unable to physically lift an electric guitar. Two sold-out acoustic concerts at New York's Carnegie Hall in December 1970 saw Young moving gingerly onto the stage, restricted by a back brace he was forced to wear. His condition would influence the sound of *After The Gold Rush*'s follow-up.

'I could only stand up four hours a day,' he told *Rolling Stone* in 1975. 'I recorded most of *Harvest* in the brace. That's a lot of the reason it's such a mellow album. 'Are You Ready For The Country?', 'Alabama' and 'Words' were all done after I had the operation. I had some discs removed.'

The Nashville sessions for *Harvest*, backed by an assemblage of country players Young christened Stray Gators, were interrupted by both the surgery and a visit to London, where critical acclaim for *After The Gold Rush* was, if anything, even more deafening than in America. Tickets for Young's show at the Royal Festival Hall sold out in two hours. After a bizarre recording session at which Young directed the London Symphony Orchestra from a bed set up beside them to avoid aggravating his back, he abruptly curtailed his visit after neighbours complained about noise at the apartment he was renting. Young indignantly caught the first flight back to America.

After completing *Harvest*, he retired to his new ranch with a new companion, actress Carrie Snodgrass. Young had contacted her through a mutual friend after seeing her in the film *Diary Of A Mad Housewife,* an incident recounted in *Harvest*'s 'A Man Needs A Maid'.

Despite the enormous success of *Harvest* and 'Heart Of Gold', the American Number 1 (10 in Britain) single it spawned, Young declined to tour immediately. Now an international superstar, he spent much of 1972 indulging his passion for film-making, shooting *Journey Through The Past*, which grew from a home movie into a sprawling, plotless mess.

Desperate for a follow-up to the multi-platinum *Harvest,* Warner Brothers agreed to fund and distribute the film if Young produced a soundtrack album, despite the fact that no one, least of all Young himself, appeared to have the slightest clue what *Journey Through The Past* was about.

It incorporated live footage of Buffalo Springfield and Crosby, Stills, Nash & Young, film of Billy Graham and Richard Nixon singing 'God Bless America', impenetrable scenes based on Young's dreams and acid hallucinations featuring an actor called Richard Lee Patterson, as well as the singer's own suggestions about improving the environment: 'like, man, y'know, rebuilding old cars instead of manufacturing new ones.' Young grandly announced that the film was influenced by Godard and Fellini.

Meanwhile, Carrie Snodgrass became pregnant. Money,

fame, kids on the way and a record company willing to indulge his every artistic whim: it should have been an idyllic time, but, once again, the darkness was about to descend.

Zeke Snodgrass Young was born on September 8, 1972. Within a few months, it became apparent that the boy had serious physical problems, eventually diagnosed as mild cerebral palsy. Warner Brothers pulled out of *Journey Through The Past*'s distribution, but released the confused mass of lo-fi live recordings, orchestral pieces and spoken-word material that made up the soundtrack anyway, blatantly promoting it as Young's follow-up to *Harvest*. A critical mauling and poor sales greeted its November release.

The same month, Young regrouped Stray Gators at La Honda, his ranch in San Mateo County, to rehearse for a 65-date, three-month tour. There was one notable addition to the line-up. After gaining assurances from his family that Danny Whitten had quit heroin, Young invited the Crazy Horse guitarist to join them. It was to prove a disastrous decision.

Whitten was the last musician to turn up at Young's ranch. He had kept his promise to quit heroin, but was staving off his withdrawal symptoms with copious quantities of alcohol and other drugs. His playing was impossibly erratic.

'We were rehearsing with him and he just couldn't cut it,' Young explained. 'He couldn't remember anything, he was too out of it. I had to tell him to go back to LA: "It's not happening man, you're not together enough." He just said, "I've got nowhere else to go, man. How am I going to tell my friends?" And he split. That night, the coroner called me from LA and told me he'd OD'd. That blew my mind, fucking blew my mind. I loved Danny. I felt responsible.'

Young's management had given Whitten a plane ticket home and $50. He used the cash to buy the heroin which killed him. He was 29 years old.

Young could not bring himself to hire a replacement guitarist.

The tour went ahead in January 1973, for it was too profitable to cancel. Seeing the full houses every night, the band and road crew lobbied for a wage increase.

'That turned Neil against everything,' said Elliot Roberts. 'He didn't know how to handle his friends hitting on him for more money. He rebelled against the success, started to see what it did to people.'

Young began drinking heavily. He refused to play the hits from *Harvest* and *After The Gold Rush*, confronting the stadium audiences with discordant, bleak new material. Fans booed and walked out. Young began screaming at them from the stage, telling them to wake up.

'It just seemed like [Whitten's death] really stood for a lot of what was going on,' Young told British music weekly *Melody Maker* in 1985. 'It was like after the freedom of the '60s and free love and drugs and everything, this is your bill. Friends, young kids dying, kids that didn't even know what they were fucking around with. It hit me pretty hard so at that time I did sort of exorcise myself.'

With his voice increasingly ruined by throat nodes, he sent out a desperate SOS to David Crosby and Graham Nash. They joined the tour as backing vocalists in Tucson, Arizona. It was a remarkably selfless act: Crosby's mother was dying of cancer and Nash's girlfriend had recently been murdered by her own brother. It was one of the few occasions when some of the members of Crosby, Stills, Nash & Young demonstrated the 'soul brother' camaraderie that was supposed to be their *raison d'être*.

But it was too late. The audiences were restless, the rows over money had poisoned the atmosphere backstage: even the mild-mannered Crosby narrowly avoided a fist fight with pianist Jack Nitzsche. At the final date, at the Oakland Coliseum, Young walked off-stage midway through playing 'Southern Man', announcing to general bewilderment: 'I can't do it with what's going on out there.' As he sang his anti-racist anthem, he had noticed a black policeman beating up a white fan in the front row. The ghastly irony of it all seemed to sum up how far things had gone awry. The tour ended there and then. The projected British dates were cancelled.

Young flew to Dallas for the American Film Festival premiere of *Journey Through The Past*. Despite hosting an impromptu Q&A session after the screening (in which he admitted 'it's hard to say what the movie means'), audiences were as horrified by Young's celluloid statement as they were by *Time Fades Away*, the wilfully antagonistic live album culled from the tour.

Next, there was another attempted Crosby, Stills, Nash & Young reunion, first in Hawaii, then at Young's ranch. As it foundered amid the inevitable druggy rancour, and his relationship with Carrie Snodgrass began to unravel, Young learned that Bruce Berry, a former Crosby, Stills, Nash & Young roadie sacked for his heroin-fuelled unpredictability, had also overdosed. Another pointless, wasteful death. One day, Young could face no more cocaine-addled, argumentative supergroup bullshit and turned up unannounced on the doorstep of his old producer David Briggs: 'He said, "Hey, I was just on my way to a Crosby, Stills, Nash & Young session and I just don't feel like going there. Let's go make some rock 'n' roll". So we packed our bags, came down to LA and wound up with the *Tonight's The Night* album.'

Poignantly, the *Tonight's The Night* sessions – named after the confused, despairing song Young had written about Bruce Berry's death – were held at Studio Instrument Rentals, owned by Berry's brother, Ken. Young and his band indulged in a curious combination of rigorous recording and desperate, hedonistic behaviour.

'It's funny, I remember the whole experience in black and white,' said Young. 'We'd get down to S.I.R. about 5 o'clock in the afternoon and start getting high, drinking tequila and playing pool. About midnight, we'd start playing. And we played Bruce and Danny on their way all through the night. I'm not a junkie and I won't even try it out to check what it's like but we all got high enough, right out there on the edge where we felt wide open to the mood.'

'They were playing and playing and playing, recording every-thing,' wrote Young's father, Scott, who attended the sessions and whose book *Neil and Me* is self-explanatorily titled. 'It was like a wake.'

When Elliot Roberts and Reprise Records heard the emo-tionally hopeless, sloppily played results, they was horrified: After *Journey Through The Past* and *Time Fades Away,* this would surely bury Young's career for good. Roberts convinced his charge that *Tonight's The Night* was unreleasable. But he could not stop Young taking the material on the road.

The reaction to another tour showcasing unreleased songs far removed from the amiable acoustic melancholy of *Harvest* was even more vociferous and negative than that which had greet-ed *Time Fades Away.* 'Play something good!' screamed one fan when the tour lurched tipsily into Manchester, England, some time later. The *Time Fades Away* tour, however, had been con-fused and nervous. This time, despite all appearances to the contrary, Young knew exactly what he was doing. He adopted the persona of a sleazy nightclub MC: 'Welcome to Miami Beach, ladies and gentlemen,' he would announce night-ly, regardless of the venue's location. 'Everything's cheaper than it looks.'

He would stretch the song 'Tonight's The Night' out for 35 minutes, play it two or three times in every set, invoke Berry's ghost with lengthy monologues ('You took Crosby's guitar and stuck it in your arm, man!'), give the audience marijuana recipes and down wine glasses full of tequila. At the Roxy in Los Angeles, he ordered a round of drinks for the entire audi-ence. He appeared so dishevelled and crazed that most onlook-ers assumed he was headed the same way as Whitten. In mid-October, BBC radio news actually announced that Young had died of a drug overdose.

Nothing could have been further from the truth. Young

recovered from the *Tonight's The Night* tour, refreshed enough to buy a new home in Malibu Beach, record an album his record company would actually release – the superb *On The Beach,* every bit as depressing as the shelved *Tonight's The Night,* but tightly played, with some sense of musical order re-imposed – and to contemplate yet another Crosby, Stills, Nash & Young reunion. By April 1974, the quartet had finally over-come their differences long enough to announce a three-month stadium tour, with an album to follow.

It was an excessive exercise in every sense. The concerts would stretch to four hours or more. The venues were huge, so huge half the audience couldn't hear the acoustic set, prompt-ing stern rebuttals from the band: 'Shut up!' yelled Crosby to one rowdy crowd. 'If you want to hear any more music at all, you'd better be quiet!'

Back at the hotels, there were custom-made pillowcases for each band member, hookers on the payroll and a suite open around the clock dispensing cocaine and champagne. Young, genuinely horrified by the level of indulgence, travelled sepa-rately from the vast entourage with his dog, Art.

Three months after the tour's September climax, a huge concert at Wembley Stadium, London, described by now defunct British music paper *Sounds* as 'a dream come true', Young finally sepa-rated from Carrie Snodgrass. Crosby, Stills, Nash & Young made yet another stab at recording an album, at the Record Plant in Los Angeles. Young shuddered at the memory: 'I walked in and almost immediately everybody got too drugged out and they were fighting all the time. I just knew it was going to be a drag, so I just turned around and went home.'

He recorded another unreleased album, *Homegrown,* a bleak acoustic dissection of the break-up with Snodgrass. With the album and cover art completed, Young held a listening party for his friends, playing them a reel-to-reel tape that also includ-ed the unreleased *Tonight's The Night*. By the end of the evening, The Band's Rick Danko had convinced Young that

Homegrown should be shelved and *Tonight's The Night* released in its place. Horrified, Reprise asked Young to reconsider. He refused. They asked him to remix it. 'I told them to shove it up their ass,' he said. The *Tonight's The Night* album was finally released in June 1975, complete with an insert that reprinted a negative review of the Tonight's The Night tour in Dutch: 'When someone is as sickened and fucked up as I was then, everything's in Dutch anyway,' offered Young by way of explanation.

By then, Young had hooked up once more with Crazy Horse. The band had been revitalised by the addition of new guitarist Frank 'Poncho' Sampedro, whose cheery influence permeated the recording of *Zuma,* an album named after Young's Malibu residence. One Sampedro-led drinking binge resulted in one of Young's most popular songs, 'Barstool Blues'. 'I was so drunk I woke up the next morning and it was like someone had left it for me. I couldn't remember writing it or anything, but I had the chords written out,' said the puzzled singer.

Young's upbeat mood extended long beyond the brief recording sessions that produced *Zuma.* With Crazy Horse, he played a series of low-key shows at small Californian clubs, the antithesis of Crosby, Stills, Nash & Young's stadium extravaganzas, and embarked upon a triumphant world tour during which, according to bassist Billy Talbot, 'Neil was just sparkling. I heard us playing like I knew nobody else could play. I have this tape from Japan. Compared to it, *Zuma* sounds like a bunch of guys sleeping in big, fat armchairs, smoking pipes. Whenever I feel down, I listen to that tape.'

The grim memory of Crosby, Stills, Nash & Young's 'doom tour' erased, Young also began playing gigs around California with Stephen Stills. Buoyed by their success, the duo began planning a collaborative album and Stills had gleefully told one audience 'the spirit of Buffalo Springfield is back!' His words were to prove horribly prophetic.

Initially, all went well. Lengthy sessions took place before Young decided to invite Crosby and Nash along in April 1976. The duo eagerly agreed, holding up work on their own collaborative album, *Whistling Down The Wire*, to join Young and Stills. Several tracks, including a couple of Nash songs, were completed in surprising harmony, before Crosby and Nash left to remix the overdue *Whistling Down The Wire*. They vowed to return as quickly as possible.

During their absence, however, Young and Stills, concerned at the pressure of performing new Crosby, Stills, Nash & Young material without the others on the forthcoming The Stills-Young Band tour, decided to wipe Crosby and Nash's vocals from the master tape. Their reaction was understandably livid, not helped by Stills's bumptious explanation that Crosby and Nash 'weren't hungry enough'.

'Fuck 'em,' snapped the peace-loving Nash in response. 'I'll go for any break, but man, it was dirty. I will not work with them again.'

The Stills-Young Band then headed out on tour, to a mixed response. The performances were erratic, and much criticism was levelled at Stills's off-key vocals. After the seventeenth show, in Charlotte, Virginia, Young's tour bus vanished into the night, never to return. The next day, while waiting forlornly for Young to arrive in Atlanta, Stills received a telegram. 'Dear Stephen, funny how things that start spontaneously end that way. Eat a peach. Neil.' The tour was over.

The official line was that Young was suffering from throat problems. Later, he offered a more prosaic explanation: 'The reviews were playing us off each other. Stephen was reading the reviews, I was trying not to read the reviews, but even the headlines were, like, Young's Hot, Stills Not. Then Stephen started thinking that other people on the tour were against him, trying to make him look bad.'

Stills, aghast at Young's departure, rashly told the press, 'I have no future,' before returning, 'his hat in his hand' to seek forgiveness from Crosby and Nash. Young vanished into the studio to record yet another unreleased album, *Chrome Dreams,* a collection of acoustic and electric tracks including 'Like A Hurricane', 'Captain Kennedy', 'Stringman' and 'Will To Love'. Young emerged in November for a brief tour with Crazy Horse and a 'fried' guest appearance performing 'Helpless' at The Band's farewell concert, filmed by Martin Scorsese as *The Last Waltz.* Scorsese was later forced to remove one backstage sequence during which a large lump of cocaine fell from Young's nose.

In a final indignity, *Whistling Down The Wire* had easily out-sold The Stills-Young Band's *Long May You Run.* Bickering, in-fighting, backstabbing and Young's swift departure: Stills had been right about the venture from the start. The spirit of Buffalo Springfield was indeed back.

By April 1977, Young had been introduced to session singer Nicolette Larson by mutual friend Linda Ronstadt. The three began rehearsing some country songs Young had written after deciding to shelve *Chrome Dreams.* Unbeknownst to Larson and Ronstadt, Young taped the rehearsals and released them in June as the first side of the uneven *American Stars 'n' Bars* album. After its release, a rumour began to spread through Californian music circles that Young was performing several nights a week, unbilled, in bars around Santa Cruz. The rumour proved to be true.

After a chance meeting at former Moby Grape leader Jerry Miller's birthday party, Young had accepted local guitarist Jeff Blackburn's invitation to join his band as lead guitarist, playing alongside former Moby Grape bassist Bob Mosley and drummer Johnny Craviotta. When local Santa Cruz paper *The Good Times* interviewed the band, they announced they were called The Ducks, and would perform only in local clubs, with tickets priced at less than $3.

Three or four nights a week, the band played sets split

equally between Young material (including a version of 'Mr. Soul' which Young pronounced 'better than Buffalo Springfield') and contributions from Blackburn and Mosley. Young, clearly enjoying himself, would crack corny duck puns onstage – 'you won't believe it when you see the bill' etc, etc – and, after the gig, would chat to the audience at the bar.

Despite his protestations to the local press, Young clearly had larger, if nebulous, plans for The Ducks. As the summer wore on, large mobile recording vans appeared outside Ducks concerts and video cameras were spotted onstage. After seven weeks, however, the national press picked up on the story. Gigs became crowded with curious out-of-towners, shouting the usual requests for 'Cinnamon Girl' and 'Southern Man'. Record companies sent scouts. There was a burglary at the house Young rented.

In what was becoming a time-honoured conclusion to his musical ventures, Young abruptly vanished, taking his son Zeke on a cross-country trip in his tour bus. They ended up in Nashville, where Young decided to record *Comes A Time*, the spiritual heir to both *Harvest*'s mellow country and western sound and its sales figures.

On its release in October 1978, *Comes A Time* was Young's biggest album in seven years. The Gone With The Wind Orchestra, the 22-piece band who performed on the album, played an outdoor Miami benefit for children's hospitals on Young's 32nd birthday.

At the end of 1977, a *Rolling Stone* reporter found Young living with Nicolette Larson, singing along with *Comes A Time* in front of the fire. Such scenes of domestic contentment were not to last for long: by January 1978, they had split, and Young began dating Pegi Morton, who lived near to his Malibu beach home. They were married in August that year.

With *Comes A Time*'s release held up by a pressing fault (Young bought back $160,000-worth of faulty copies to prevent them reaching the stores), he had become musically restless again. On a visit to England the previous year, he had seen the tumult caused by punk rock.

'Kids were tired of the rock stars and the limousines and the abusing of stage privileges as stars,' he noted approvingly, perhaps recollecting the decadent horror of Crosby, Stills, Nash & Young's 1974 tour. 'There was new music the kids were listening to. As soon as I heard my contemporaries saying, "God, what the fuck is this? This is going to be over in three months," I knew it was a sure sign right there that they're going to bite it if they don't watch out. Punk music, new wave, call it what you want. It's still rock 'n' roll to me, it's still the basis of what's going on.'

While working on his second film, *Human Highway*, in which Young played himself and his friend Dean Stockwell played his manager, he had been introduced to Akron new-wave band Devo. In early June, he arranged a private gig at San Francisco punk club Mabuhay Gardens, where Devo performed his new song, a paean to the Sex Pistols and the longevity of rock 'n' roll called 'My My, Hey Hey (Out Of The Blue)', for a nightmare sequence in the movie. During the song, he noticed two members of Devo chanting 'rust never sleeps', a slogan they had devised while working in advertising to promote a rust-remover. It became the name of Young's next tour, an extravaganza which opened on September 18.

It featured roadies dressed as Star Wars Jawas, taped announcements from the Woodstock festival blaring through the speakers and Crazy Horse playing at ear-splitting volume ('I wanted people to leave saying Neil Young's show was the loudest fucking thing they'd ever heard'), dwarfed by a set of outsized microphones and amplifiers. It was, declared Young, symbolic of the size of the music industry itself. 'Somebody like Foreigner or Boston, they come out with a record and sell ten times what I do. I think that's great. But I still feel like this little guy.'

The show at San Francisco's Cow Palace was filmed and released as *Rust Never Sleeps*, directed by Young under his and

Stockwell's Bernard Shakey pseudonym. He claimed that if audiences watched the film through the special Rust-O-Vision glasses provided, they could see chunks of rust falling from his guitar as he played older songs. Nothing of the sort was true, of course, but it was a nice metaphor for punk's re-energising effect on his career.

Yet again, however, personal tragedy was to overshadow artistic success. On October 23, 1978 Young's Malibu home burned down as he played the penultimate show of the tour at The Forum, Los Angeles. Then, in November that year, Young's second son Ben was born. Within a few months, he, as with Zeke, was diagnosed with cerebral palsy. Horribly, the Youngs learned the diagnosis by overhearing a conversation between two doctors in the hospital waiting room.

'It was too big a picture to comprehend,' said Young. 'Pegi's heartbroken, we're both shocked. I couldn't believe it. There are two different mothers. I remember looking at the sky, looking for a sign, wondering "What the fuck is going on? Why are the kids in this situation? What the hell caused this? What did I do? There must be something wrong with me."'

But it was not a genetic condition, just a terrible coincidence. While the *Rust Never Sleeps* album and the *Live Rust* double set rode critical plaudits into the album chart, the couple began an exhaustive search for help in alleviating Ben's condition. Worse was to follow: in March 1980, Pegi was diagnosed with a brain tumour. Initially, she was given only a 50 per cent chance of survival, but two months later, surgery proved successful. The domestic pressures, however, were taking their toll on Young's career.

'I made up my mind I was gonna take care of Pegi, take care of the kids,' he remembered years later. 'We were gonna go on, we weren't gonna be selfish. I wasn't gonna hurt. I closed myself down so much that I was doing great with surviving, but my soul was completely encased. I didn't even consider that I would need a soul to play my music, that when I shut the door on pain, I shut the door on my music. That's what I did.'

Young played live only once between 1979 and 1982. His next album, *Hawks And Doves*, released in January 1981, was unremarkable by comparison to *Rust Never Sleeps*, interesting more for Young's lyrical affirmations of faith in his family – 'we don't back down from no trouble, we do get up in the morning,' he sang on Coastline – than its anaemic musical content. In December, he released *Re-Ac-Tor*, a Crazy Horse album inspired by The Program, the Institute Of Human Potential's method of teaching handicapped children, in which Ben was enrolled.

'You manipulate the kid through a crawling pattern,' explained Young. 'You're brainwashed to think the only thing that you can do that's gonna save your kid is this program, and they have you so scared that if they call and you're not at the house, you're off the program, forget it. You've ruined it for your kid. We lasted 18 months: 18 months of not going out, 18 months of not doing anything. And during those months I made *Re-Ac-Tor*.'

The album was shorn of melody and, like The Program itself, gruellingly repetitious. The members of Crazy Horse were forced to record during the few hours a day Young was freed from his son's therapy. 'We weren't used to being in the studio at 10 in the morning and playing rock 'n' roll,' admitted Ralph Molina. 'We were going through our little drug thing at the time.'

Hawks And Doves and *Re-Ac-Tor* met with commercial indifference: the public understandably declining to listen to Young singing 'Got mashed potatoes, ain't got no T-bone' over and over again for 10 minutes, however much it reflected his personal turmoil.

Shortly after removing Ben from The Program in February 1982, Young left Reprise and signed with former Crosby, Stills, Nash & Young manager David Geffen's Geffen label. It was supposed to be a new beginning, but problems surfaced almost immediately, when Young submitted *Island In The Sun*, an album in the gently commercial vein of *Harvest* and *Comes A Time*.

'They advised me not to put it out,' said Young. 'Because it was my first record for Geffen, I thought, "Well, this is a fresh, new thing. He's got some new ideas." It didn't really register to me that I was being manipulated. Until the second record.'

The 'second record' was to be the most radical of Young's career. He had long been interested in the music of German synthesizer pioneers Kraftwerk – their former percussionist Karl Bartos recalls spending an evening at Young's ranch in the mid-1970s, where the band's suits and short hair presented an amusing contrast with Young's dishevelled appearance – and his purchase of a vocoder voice synthesizer in 1981 had inspired a new set of electronic-based songs, utterly unlike anything Young had produced before. The resulting album, *Trans*, was based around a confusing concept inspired by the technology used to alleviate Ben's disability.

'*Trans* was all about these robot-humanoid people working in this hospital and one thing they were trying to do was teach this little baby to push a button,' said Young in the late 1980s. '*Trans* is the beginning of my search for communication with a severely handicapped, non-oral person. 'Transformer Man' is a song for my kid with his little button and his train set and his transformer. The whole thing is for Ben. People completely misunderstood *Trans*, but they didn't have a fuckin' chance in the world, it was very obscure. *Trans* is about communication, but it's not getting through. You can't understand the words on *Trans* and I can't understand my son's words. So feel that.'

With Ben's new therapy less intense and demanding, Young could tour again. Before the album's release, he assembled the Trans Band, recruiting Bruce Palmer on bass, who had spent the years since Buffalo Springfield living off his meagre royalties in a Sikh commune in Toronto. As with The Stills-Young Band debacle, echoes of Buffalo Springfield's turbulent career began appearing almost immediately. Within two months of his arrival in May 1982, Palmer had been sacked because of a drinking problem, only to be reinstated in August.

'People that feel good to play with are hard to find,' Young remarked. 'Usually I like people who are extremely erratic.'

The *Trans* European tour came complete with Young sporting short hair and skinny tie à la Kraftwerk and vocoder-heavy new tracks such as 'Sample and Hold' and 'Computer Age' jostling for position among crowd-pleasing old favourites. Even the 'acoustic' solo tour which followed *Trans*'s release in January 1983 featured synth-drums and synchronised video footage.

'Neil Young from the 1960s and early '70s is like Perry Como,' he snapped defiantly, when asked about his new direction, adding a pointed 'If I was still taking that seriously, I'd be where Crosby, Stills & Nash are today.'

He had a point. In the early 1980s, Crosby, Stills & Nash looked increasingly anachronistic, sporadically hawking 'Teach Your Children' and 'Almost Cut My Hair' around America's arenas, with David Crosby's horrific addiction to freebase cocaine proof in itself that the Woodstock era they still mythologised was long gone. But for all its futuristic risk-taking, *Trans* had easily been outsold by Crosby, Stills & Nash's lacklustre *Daylight Again*. A hint of doubt began to appear in Young's pronouncements: 'Computer music, I think it's going to be my future,' he told one confused reporter. 'Although it may not be.'

In fact, Young had already prepared a follow-up album by the time he collapsed from exhaustion 45 minutes into a show in Louisville, Kentucky, abruptly ending the solo tour. As with *Island In The Sun*, *Old Ways* was an attempt to recreate Young's most successful era. The album was recorded in Nashville with a combination of musicians from *Harvest* and *Comes A Time*. And as with *Island In The Sun*, it was rejected outright by Geffen.

'I was so stoked about that record,' fumed Young. 'I sent Geffen a tape of it that had eight songs on it. I called them up a week later, because I hadn't heard anything and they said "Well, frankly Neil, this record scares us a lot. We don't think this is the right direction for you to be going in." I guess they just saw me as some old hippie from the '60s still trying to make acoustic music or something.'

Shaken by a second rejection in two years, the uncompromising Young of the mid-1970s, the Young who had screamed at his audiences to wake the fuck up and insisted on touring *Tonight's The Night* two years before its release suddenly re-emerged. 'They wanted more rock 'n' roll,' he recalled. 'OK, fine. I'll give you some rock 'n' roll. I almost vindictively gave them *Everybody's Rockin'*.'

Everybody's Rockin', a collection of ersatz rockabilly Young had primarily written to amuse his wife, had been recorded with The Shocking Pinks, a new backing band featuring former Steppenwolf guitarist Larry Byrom alongside Craig Hayes, a Nashville lawyer who contributed saxophone under the pseudonym Vito Toledo. The album was short – under 25 minutes – primarily because Geffen had cut the sessions short, horrified at the music that was emerging. Those who bothered to buy the finished product could usually see Geffen's point.

The *Everybody's Rockin'* tracks worked well as part of a light-hearted second set during Young's second American tour of 1983, complete with a group of high-kicking dancing girls fronted by Pegi Young and Young himself sporting a white suit and authentically greasy quiff. As an album, they sounded hopelessly flat, a commercial and artistic nadir just four years after the Top Ten success of *Comes A Time* and *Rust Never Sleeps*.

Young remained defiant, blaming Geffen for the album's failure ('They decided "That record's not gonna get noticed, we're gonna press as few of those as possible and not do anything."'), cutting short one date of the tour that followed the album's release because the Michigan audience 'didn't deserve The Shocking Pinks', and making a 90-minute documentary about the band which never saw the light of day. *Everybody's Rockin'* remained a touchy subject for years.

Discussing the album in 1995, Young snapped: 'What am I? Stupid? Did people really think I put that out thinking it was the greatest fucking thing I ever recorded? Obviously I'm aware it's not. It was a way of further destroying what I'd already set up.'

Young turned back to Crazy Horse, with whom he played two Santa Cruz shows in February, debuting fast, angry, simple new material, tracks called 'Rock Forever' and 'Violent Side'. A disastrous recording session with additional horn players put paid to any hopes of a new collaborative album. 'It ended up a big fuckin' bum-out because we had never failed so completely to get anything,' lamented Young. 'Crazy Horse didn't do anything for a long time after that.'

In the 1980s, whenever recording sessions collapsed or albums bombed, Young returned to the one area he was guaranteed success: touring America's arenas. He assembled a new band to play country music, The International Harvesters, featuring longstanding Young sidemen Tim Drummond and Ben Keith among their ranks. They toured America throughout 1984, defiantly playing tracks from the rejected *Old Ways* album alongside new songs including 'Amber Jean', Young's ode to his new daughter, born on 15 May 1984. This time, there was no terrible discovery months after birth: Young proudly announced she was 'growing like a little flower should', free from cerebral palsy.

If Young had reached a new level of domestic contentment, his professional life was becoming increasingly convoluted and complex. By September, Geffen, vastly unamused by the sight of Young and band performing at the Grand Ole Opry, duetting with Willie Nelson and Waylon Jennings and appearing on Nashville Now, had launched a $3,000,000 lawsuit against him, accusing him of making deliberately 'unrepresentative' albums. '[David Geffen] took it personally when I handed him a straight country or rockabilly album,' said an injured Young. 'He thought I was making those albums to laugh at him, as a joke at his expense.'

Young's response was simple and devastatingly effective: 'I told them the longer you sue me for making country music, the longer I'm going to play country music. Either you back off or I'm going to play country music forever. And then you won't be able to sue me anymore because country music will be what I always do, so it won't be uncharacteristic anymore, hahaha. So stop telling me what to do or I'll turn into George Jones.'

The tour rolled truculently on throughout 1985, interrupted only by a brief Australasian tour with Crazy Horse – Tim Drummond declined to tour as his wife was about to give birth, effectively stopping the intended International Harvesters appearance – and a brief and dreadful appearance with Crosby, Stills & Nash at Live Aid.

David Crosby's freebase addiction was still at its height. A string of busts had led to a stay at a New Jersey rehab clinic, which ended dramatically when Crosby climbed the walls of the hospital and escaped. Busted again, he had endured a three-month jail sentence in March 1985, which, despite his protestations to the contrary, had done nothing to curb his addiction.

At Live Aid, Crosby's Hogarthian physical appearance and performance was so bad, even his best friend Nash told reporters, 'He'll eventually die. It's only a question of when.' Young was similarly appalled, dismissing the Live Aid appearance as 'an exception to the rule' that he would not perform with the trio until Crosby had cleaned up: 'I will not go out with them, have everyone scrutinise the band, how big it is and how much it meant, and see this guy that's so fucked up on drugs. Some young kid 12 years old, why should he see Crosby, Stills, Nash & Young on TV and know that this guy's a cocaine addict, been freebasing for fuckin' years and years and years and he looks like a vegetable, but they're still on TV and they're still making it and they're still big stars? I don't wanna show anybody that.'

If the Live Aid appearance was lacklustre, however, the charity event itself had a lasting effect on Young. A few weeks later, while making a video with Willie Nelson for their duet, 'Are There Any More Real Cowboys?', Young suggested a similar event could be staged to benefit American farmers, then struggling through appalling financial hardship. Farm Aid eventually took place on September 22, opening with Young and Nelson's duet and going on to raise $9,000,000. Young even went to Washington to lobby senators on the farmers' behalf.

It was not Young's only political statement of the year. In interviews around the August release of *Old Ways*, a schlocky collection of Nashville-friendly country that confirmed Geffen's worst fears, Young began espousing pro-Reagan sentiments, an unthinkable move from the man Vice-President Spiro Agnew had condemned for writing 'Ohio'.

'I stand behind Reagan when it comes to build-up [of nuclear weapons],' he announced to one reporter, 'to stand, to be able to play hardball with other countries that are aggressive towards free countries. I don't think there's anything wrong with that.'

It was further damage to a career already in freefall. As new American bands such as The Long Ryders and Green On Red began to display how the influence of Young's 1970s records had seeped through to a new generation, the man himself looked hopelessly disconnected, making MOR country albums and arguing for more nuclear weapons.

Meanwhile, his battles with Geffen continued apace. While the 'unrepresentative music' lawsuit was quietly dropped after 18 months – 'David Geffen called me up one day and said "I'm wrong, we shouldn't have done it and it didn't work." And I said, "Too right you're wrong",' Young recalled with satisfaction – the label refused to release a five-track Farm Aid benefit EP. The story was somewhat overshadowed by the news that David Crosby, after another drug bust and two weeks on the run without money or shoes, had finally given himself up to Florida police. He was to spend the next seven months in prison.

Young, meanwhile, spent 1986 treading water. He reworked the songs from the aborted Crazy Horse sessions two years earlier into the hopelessly over-produced *Landing On Water*, another dud album released in July. He re-formed Crazy Horse, billing them as The Third Best Garage Band In The World, and toured America with them on a set designed to look like a garage: it was dubbed The Rusted Out Garage Tour.

The name was not the only echo of the *Rust Never Sleeps* era. Once again, Young decided to film the tour, depositing two video-8 cameras backstage and in hotels and encouraging band members and crew to talk directly to them. They obliged, but what emerged was, in Young's words, 'dark as hell': Crazy Horse had little in the way of new material and their playing was affected by Billy Talbot's increasing dependence on alcohol. The resulting friction between band members was unflinchingly documented in the unreleased film, *Muddy Track*.

The band also taped what little new material the tour had, overdubbing it in the studio, as they had a decade previously with *Rust Never Sleeps*. As an attempt to recapture former glories, it was a failure. The resulting *Life* album, while a considerable improvement on *Landing On Water* and *Old Ways*, was nevertheless the weakest Crazy Horse album to date. When the tour moved on to Europe in early 1987, the band played to half-empty halls and faced a string of cancellations because of poor ticket sales in Switzerland and France.

In America, regular tours had kept fans satisfied in a way that Young's recent albums could not. In Europe, where he had not toured since 1982 (tours in 1984 and 1986 had been scheduled, then mysteriously cancelled), the damage caused to Young's reputation both by *Old Ways* and *Landing On Water* and his pro-nuclear, pro-Reagan pronouncements could not be underestimated. The audience in Milan rioted, while in Frankfurt, Young was hit by a glass. It was, he later admitted, 'a bad period for us.'

The only genuine rays of hope seemed to come from the past. Young participated in a brief but good-humoured reunion of The Squires as part of a Winnipeg rock 'n' roll festival, and when David Crosby quietly emerged from a Texas prison in

August 1986, clean-shaven and finally free of drugs, Young kept good his promise to work with Crosby, Stills & Nash again. The quartet performed alongside Bruce Springsteen, Tom Petty and Don Henley in Mountain View, California in October. The occasion was the first Bridge Concert, organised by Pegi Young to raise funds for a handicapped children's school in San Francisco. It would become a yearly event and the charity with which Young was most closely associated.

They also planned to record an album, but initially found their efforts blocked, ironically by their former manager and Young's current label head David Geffen. Crosby, Stills & Nash were still signed to Atlantic, and Geffen announced, 'If they want to make a record with Neil Young, that record can only be made for me, because I will not allow Neil to make a record for anybody while he's under exclusive contract for me.'

Despite the quartet's bravado about their re-formation ('there's a very strong chance of the group being better and stronger and perhaps bigger than it was before,' claimed Young), the situation with Geffen was only resolved when Young released *Life*, the final album of his contract, and began negotiating a contract with his old label Reprise, part of the same group as Atlantic. It was the end of an appalling relationship between artist and label.

'Elliot Roberts called me and told me,' said a jubilant Young. 'I had just smoked this big bomber and I nearly had a heart attack.'

Years later, he was still smarting at his treatment, claiming loudly that REM had refused to sign to Geffen because of the lawsuit against him. More difficult to resolve was the quartet's latest problem: Stephen Stills was now in the grip of freebase addiction. His behaviour during the sessions for *American Dream*, the first Crosby, Stills, Nash & Young album since 1970, disturbed all concerned. Despite the fact that he was in the presence of a recovering addict, Stills's freebase paraphernalia was often clearly visible. Young acidly remarked that the album should be titled *Songs For Balding Baseheads*, and ploughed grimly ahead with the sessions at his ranch studio.

After the album was completed, Young refused to tour with the trio or even perform with them at the Atlantic Records 40th birthday concert in New York. In interview, he began referring to Stills in terms that one year previously had been used to describe Crosby. 'He's got a lot of monkeys on his back and they're not letting them do his thing,' he told *Rolling Stone*. 'I just hope he makes it.'

By then, Young's solo career had undergone a mild transformation of fortune. On an American tour to promote *Life* in August 1987, he had begun performing two songs with Crazy Horse augmented by their saxophone-playing roadie, Larry Cragg. It was, Young claimed, the only part of the evening he enjoyed. 'The crowd seemed to like it too,' he observed. 'They were going fucking nuts and no-one was shouting for 'Southern Man' like they've done throughout my whole fucking career.'

Next, he assembled a six-piece horn section to augment Crazy Horse, christened them The Bluenotes, wrote a whole new set of blues-based material and toured it around California. He refused to play old material. Occasionally, he had hecklers thrown out of the gigs. He recorded an album with The Bluenotes, and commissioned a video for its title track, 'This Note's For You', from maverick director Julien Temple. Temple, who had been responsible for The Rolling Stones' banned 'Undercover Of The Night' promo, set about satirising recent product endorsements by Michael Jackson and Whitney Houston. The video was first banned, then embraced and regularly screened by MTV.

Young was still playing roles – just as the bequiffed leader of The Shocking Pinks had been a 'fictional' character Young played onstage, so the leader of The Bluenotes was a character called Shakey Deal – but some of the fire that had powered him throughout the 1970s appeared to be returning.

Its intensity was doubled after the debacle of the Crosby, Stills, Nash & Young reunion. He reconvened The Bluenotes – Frank 'Poncho' Sampedro was the solitary member of Crazy Horse who remained in the line-up – and by August 1988 they were touring America again, with a set packed with fresh material including 'Sixty To Zero', a lengthy, angry catalogue of contemporary American woes. Their performances became more confrontational. Young would tear all the strings from his guitar, kick microphone stands off-stage, berate the audience for their lack of response to his new material. 'Well, that was then,' he snapped at the audience in Jones Beach after performing a desultory 'After The Gold Rush'.

Among Young's new songs was 'Cocaine Eyes', a devastating attack on Stephen Stills's drug-bloated condition. It was one of the tracks he recorded with The Bluenotes' drummer and bass player – dubbed The Restless or The Lost Dogs when they formed a two-man backing group – in New York in November 1988.

The sessions were meant to produce a new album, *Times Square*, but its disturbing mix of howled vocals and guitars ruptured with feedback was so uncommercial that Young declined to release it. 'I changed my mind about it because I thought I really wanted to release an album that would have an effect, that wasn't just gonna be something I wanted to do,' he explained. 'If you don't have a record they can play on the radio, then you might as well forget it.'

Instead, the five most sonically extreme tracks were assembled as *Eldorado*, a mini-album released only in Japan and Australasia during Young's April 1989 tour of those territories. A year previously, Young had wondered aloud in interview about his continued relevance as a rock artist: 'How long can you keep doing it and really do it? Or do you become a reenactment of an earlier happening?'

His questions were answered both by two releases – *Eldorado*, a record as vigorous and challenging as anything American rock had produced in the 1980s, and *The Bridge*, a compilation of Young covers by the cream of the current alternative rock scene. It simply reiterated a fact that had been audible for some time: Young's shadow hung heavy over some of the best young bands currently operating in America. Most contributors were simply repaying a stylistic debt to Young. Soul Asylum, The Flaming Lips, Pixies and Dinosaur Jr's sounds all used some combination of open-tuned guitars, ear-splitting solos and high-pitched vocals, clearly influenced by Crazy Horse. Indeed, Dinosaur Jr sounded so like Crazy Horse that they delivered a wisecracking heavy-metal parody of 'Lotta Love' for the album: if they had covered a Young song in their usual style, it would have been indistinguishable from the original. To Sonic Youth, Young was a figure from rock's margins with a tendency towards impenetrable avant-garde statements, and a healthily punk rock attitude to the commercial demands of the music industry. Their contribution, tellingly, was a radical reconstruction of *Trans's* 'Computer Age'. For Australia's Nick Cave, whose remarkable, stately version of 'Helpless' was a highlight, Young was simply a classic songwriter.

It was all high praise, and the proceeds went to the Youngs' Bridge School charity, but the man himself reacted as unpredictably as ever. For Young, the covers on *The Bridge* were a challenge from the younger generation. 'It's nice that they did that tribute album, but I'm not ready for it,' he commented, as ornery as ever. 'They don't mean to close the book, but to me it's still threatening.'

Three months later – after ironically scooping MTV's Music Video Of The Year Award for 'This Note's For You' – came Young's response. Like *Rust Never Sleeps* and *Tonight's The Night*, *Freedom* opened and closed with the same track: 'Rockin' In The Free World', a rather troubled song about the state of America that suddenly took on new resonances when state socialism collapsed in Eastern Europe shortly after its release.

Freedom was the first entirely consistent album Young had released in a decade. He was fêted with a string of television specials and documentaries in the USA and Canada. New bands kept emerging bearing the mark of his influence. Seattle's Mudhoney and Nirvana not only took Crazy Horse's sludgy, stoned blueprint as their own, but, more incredibly, adopted Young's wardrobe of plaid shirts and ripped jeans. Young responded to his commercial and critical resurgence by lambasting any interviewer who dared suggest he'd made a comeback, instead positing the theory that the chaos of his career in the 1980s had all been part of the plan.

'Listen,' he growled at Nick Kent in late 1989, 'I don't have to come back because I've never been gone! They write stuff like "Oh, this year Neil Young's OK again." Fuck them! I don't need them to tell me if I'm OK or ñot! As far as I'm concerned, I've always been OK! I'm not some '60s band coming back to take advantage of some wave of bullshit nostalgia,' he added, not without reason. 'I'm someone who's always tried systematically to destroy the very basis of my record-buying public. You destroy what you did before and you're free to carry on. So, I've been busy destroying all these things.'

For all the angry bluster in such pronouncements, Young's career path in the 1990s was considerably more straightforward than the decade that preceded it. Alongside fellow mavericks Lou Reed and Bob Dylan, he settled comfortably into the role of American rock figurehead, as Nirvana and the rest of the grunge movement awkwardly, and in Nirvana's case unwillingly, ascended to global importance. 'They've started calling me Don Grungeone,' he noted. 'I kinda got this fatherly thing happening right now. Don't ask me why. I'm just here, where I always was, doing what I love to do.'

Young played a string of benefit shows in early 1990, including an appearance at April's Nelson Mandela: An International Tribute For A Free South Africa concert at London's Wembley Stadium and a reunion with Crosby, Stills & Nash at a benefit for their former drummer Dallas Taylor, whose familiar problems with drugs and alcohol had left him requiring a liver transplant, something Crosby himself would eventually feel the need for. He then reconvened Crazy Horse, recording the album *Ragged Glory*, a return to the amped-up, freewheeling rock of *Zuma*, in his home studio. After the sessions ended in July, Young spent several months in Florida, looking after his ailing mother, Rassy. She died on October 15, the day before her 73rd birthday.

Ragged Glory had been released a month previously. It was a further claim to rebellious contemporaneity: Young was called upon to defend the obscenity-driven, but coyly asterisked 'F*!#in' Up' on MTV, while in interviews he claimed the lengthy feedback codas at the end of virtually every song were a means of irritating commercial radio stations. 'Everything now is concerned with formats. This is Fuck Your Format. Put this in your own fucking format,' he told one reporter, before adopting a glib radio DJ's voice: 'OK, that was a new song, ah, there by, ah, Neil Young. Nine and a half minutes long with a 45-fuckin'-second last note. Rilly hope you enjoyed it. Haw haw haw.'

However, the feedback finales were about to take on a more serious tone. Just as Young and Crazy Horse were about to embark on the *Ragged Glory* World Tour – an event delayed when guitarist Frank 'Poncho' Sampedro was hospitalised for an emergency appendectomy – the Gulf War broke out. Young's live audience was now so all-encompassing that he discovered both support and condemnation for the war among his fans.

'Everybody in the States was so emotionally involved with the Gulf War,' he said. 'We could see and hear it every night, on people's faces, on the TV, on the telephone. Each night the audience would be full of SUPPORT OUR TROOPS stickers, yellow ribbons and peace symbols. It was this kind of emotional explosiveness that was the real catalyst for the music.'

Young's response was to drag out songs to mammoth length, ending them with seemingly endless, searing explosions of feedback. For an audience already battered by support slots from

Sonic Youth and new wave Californians Social Distortion, Crazy Horse's set sounded less like a greatest hits selection (the outsized stage props recalled the *Rust Never Sleeps* tour) than warfare erupting onstage.

'It was intense, it was real,' Young mused. 'I could see people dying in my mind. I could see bombs falling, buildings collapsing on families. We were watching CNN all the time, watching all this shit happen and then going out to play. I feel there was nothing else I could do. As soon as the war started, I changed the set list. A few *Ragged Glory* songs were replaced with older songs I knew people could relate to. I knew people could be unified, so whatever could bring people together was more important than me playing a new song. We couldn't go out there and be just entertainment. It would have been bad taste.'

Four months of excessive volume and ear-splitting frequencies onstage eventually took their toll on the 45-year-old Young. After mixing the tapes of the tour into a double live CD, *Weld*, and an accompanying 37-minute collage of feedback called *Arc*, Young discovered he was suffering from an extreme form of tinnitus called hyperacoustis.

He was forced to cancel a three-date Japanese tour for Amnesty International, and trumpeted his decision to abandon rock music. 'I don't want to do any more of that loud stuff. It would have been like flying off into the sun,' he said, announcing that his next album, recorded almost immediately after the Ragged Glory tour had ended, was a return to homespun, *Harvest*-style folk and country. Like most of Young's sweeping pronouncements over the years, it proved to be untrue. He had, after all, announced on at least three separate occasions in the last 20 years that he would never play with Crazy Horse again, only to return to them each time.

Harvest Moon, as the new album was titled, was delayed throughout 1992. In true *Tonight's The Night* style, Young nevertheless embarked on an acoustic tour in January to promote the record. There were other, more unfortunate echoes from the past too: as with the 1974 Crosby, Stills, Nash & Young tour, Young had difficulty making himself heard over the audience's chatter. In New York, one audience member began yelling the lyrics to 'Old Man' while Young attempted to play the *Harvest Moon* track 'You and Me', prompting Young to issue a curt 'Shut up, you asshole!' Gigs in Dayton and Detroit were similarly interrupted, while a later show in Chicago was abandoned altogether. The next night at the same venue, Young insisted beer was banned from sale.

More happily, Young was awarded an Honorary Doctorate in music by Lockheed University, Thunder Bay, a ceremony attended by his father, and he played extended, acclaimed versions of 'Just Like Tom Thumb's Blues' and 'All Along The Watchtower' at Bob Dylan's 30th Anniversary Concert at Madison Square Garden, New York. Backed by house band Booker T & The MGs, Young received one of the most rapturous receptions of the evening.

As 1993 dawned, and for all his talk of 'destroying the very basis of my record-buying public', Young seemed more comfortable with his past than ever before. He had reworked his back catalogue for an *Unplugged* show, and even resolved the problems of his years with Geffen by compiling the *Lucky Thirteen* album for the label, mixing the best tracks from his 1980s albums with unreleased material. He went on a European tour with Booker T & The MGs, after two weeks of rehearsal, playing what amounted to a relatively rigid greatest hits set, his vow to quit rock music swiftly forgotten. He accepted the plaudits of the burgeoning grunge movement, jamming 'Rockin' In The Free World' with Pearl Jam at a Stockholm gig, and repeating the performance at the MTV Video Awards in September.

If Young appeared to be resting on his considerable laurels, his next album was, in its own way, as dramatic a statement as *Tonight's The Night* and *Rust Never Sleeps*. Recorded with Crazy Horse, *Sleeps With Angels* provided a mysterious, lugubrious world view, with oblique, measured performances far removed from the band's usual clodhopping approach. On its release in August 1994, most listeners assumed the album's inspiration to be Kurt Cobain, the lead singer of Nirvana who had quoted Young's 'Hey Hey, My My (Into The Black)' in his suicide note: 'It's better to burn out than to fade away'. The album had been recorded both before and after Cobain's April suicide. Young compounded the mystery by refusing to discuss either the album or Cobain in interviews, although it had been rumoured that he had tried to contact the 27-year-old in the weeks preceding his death.

'*Sleeps With Angels* has a lot of overtones to it, from different situations that were described in it. A lot of sad scenes. I've never really spoken about why I made it,' he told one journalist. 'I don't want to start now.' When the journalist suggested a connection between Cobain and Danny Whitten – there was a marked physical similarity too – Young stonewalled again: 'I just don't want to talk about that. That's my decision. I've made a choice not to talk about it and I'm sticking to it.'

Perhaps still fearful for his hearing, Young declined to tour the album, instead issuing a 27-minute video, directed by Jonathan Demme, of *Stop Making Sense* fame, and shot at Complex Recording Studios, Los Angeles in October 1994. Young and Crazy Horse performed four *Sleeps With Angels* tracks – 'My Heart', 'Prime Of Life', the lengthy 'Change Your Mind' and 'Piece Of Crap' – for the cameras. Demme's sympathetic direction led critic Paul Williams to breathlessly proclaim the video 'Neil Young and Rock 'n' Roll's Finest Moment'.

'He's taught us a lot as a band about dignity and commitment and playing in the moment,' said Pearl Jam's Eddie Vedder, inducting Young into the Rock 'n' Roll Hall Of Fame in January 1995. Young, who played a new track, 'Act Of Love', with Pearl Jam that night, was about to teach them even more.

'If you have a good situation and can make music whenever

you want with a whole bunch of people who are cool and you have nothing else to do, then ultimately, it's going to get a little shallow, because there's not enough challenge,' claimed Young, explaining his decision to write and record an entire album with Pearl Jam in four days later that month. The result was *Mirror Ball*, an album that, despite occasional shortcomings, boasted suitably loose performances and proved Young had lost little of his thirst for experimentation.

'I was just conscious of this big, smouldering mass of sound,' said Young of the finished product. Because of contractual obligations, Pearl Jam's name was not featured on the album packaging, but the band accompanied Young on yet another European tour that summer. The veteran singer was full of praise for his youthful cohorts. 'On a purely musical level, this is the first time I've seen a band with three potential lead guitarists since Buffalo Springfield,' he said. 'Plus here's Jack Irons, their drummer, who was just unbelievable. He played his ass off. I can't say enough good things about him.'

Now into his fifties, Young's productivity rate showed few signs of slowing down. Despite claiming to have never heard of director Jim Jarmusch – a peculiar state of affairs considering Young's long-standing interest in arthouse cinema – he contributed an improvised soundtrack to *Dead Man*, Jarmusch's tale of the Old West, starring Johnny Depp. He invited Jarmusch along to document the occasion when Crazy Horse toured together for the first time since the fateful *Ragged Glory* tour.

Jarmusch's cameras followed the band, touting a decidedly mixed collaborative album, *Broken Arrow*, around Europe and America. As with *Muddy Track* (which remained unreleased even when Young's barely-seen *Human Highway* finally made its way onto video in 1995, 13 years after its premiere), the results were far from the standard gushing rock biopic. Amid a mass of concert and archive footage, including the memorable sight of a profoundly stoned Crazy Horse nearly setting fire to a Glasgow hotel in 1976, the backstage scenes showed Billy

Talbot and Young engaged in a furious argument. Crazy Horse, for their part, appeared as truculent and unpredictable as their frontman. Frank 'Poncho' Sampedro was pictured openly attacking Jarmusch, loudly bemoaning the fact that a 'hip, trendy kind of New York artsy-fartsy film producer' could hope to 'scratch the tip of the iceberg with a couple of cute questions'.

'Don't you have friction in your job?' asked Young when it was pointed out that some of the footage was less than flattering. 'Aren't there some assholes that you can't get along with? It's part of the music, part of being in a group, part of being brothers. Despite the fighting, we all care about the same thing.'

Nevertheless, Young and Crazy Horse declined to attend the film's showing at the San Francisco Film Festival and avoided the party afterwards, preferring instead to play a gig together across town at the Trocadero Transfer.

After the fuss surrounding *Year Of The Horse* had died down, Young appeared to keep a low profile for the remainder of the decade. Reprise claimed that he was working on another solo album in the acoustic *Harvest Moon* vein, indicating that Young's career had finally settled into something approaching a routine: electric album and tour followed by acoustic album and solo tour. He had started his own label, Vapor, with Elliot Roberts in 1996, signing, of all people, Jonathan Richman, one of the few figures in American rock with a claim to be as bloody-minded as Young himself. Young came out in vocal support of the usual Farm Aid causes, speaking out against genetically modified foods, and appeared at a handful of charity gigs in 1998, sporting a grey beard and jamming with Grateful Dead pretenders Phish at that year's Bridge benefit. His place as one of American rock's figureheads was secure. 'Wow, Neil Young just introduced us,' said an awestruck E, lead singer of Eels, at the same event. 'Now what do we do?'

With Young, however, there was always room for some controversy. Buffalo Springfield were inducted into the Rock 'n'

49

Roll Hall Of Fame in October 1997, but Young, who had put a stop to a mooted Springfield reunion after only one rehearsal nine years previously, failed to turn up. The problem was not, he claimed, his fellow band members, all present and correct at the ceremony. It was the presence of music satellite channel VH-1, who for the first time were broadcasting an edited version of the show.

'Inductees are severely limited in the amount of guests they can bring,' Young wrote in an open letter to the US press. 'They are forced to be on a TV show, for which they are not paid, and whatever comments they would like to make, dirty laundry they would like to air, thanks they would like to give, are all subject to the VH-1 editor, someone who has absolutely no right to interfere.'

The echoes of Young's first departure from Buffalo Springfield on the eve of their appearance on the Johnny Carson Show were unmistakable. 'Neil's an interesting fellow, man,' remarked a tactful Richie Furay, now a Christian minister. 'You never know quite how to read him.'

Furay's comments were borne out in 1999, when, after a lengthy solo acoustic tour – far better-humoured than the 1992 outing – Young announced that he would be participating in a new Crosby, Stills, Nash & Young album, eleven years after the mediocre *American Dream*. The interim period had seen Crosby, Stills & Nash make an uninspired album, 1990's *Live It Up*, interspersed with solo records of varying quality for ever-smaller labels. Crosby had become something of a media celebrity, thanks to chat show appearances and roles in sitcoms like Rosanne, but had also undergone a liver transplant in 1994. 'I don't think we've made a decent record since 1977's CSN,' commented a doleful but prosaic Stills.

'They didn't have a record company, they were actually in the studio on their own,' recalled Young. 'They wanted to make their music more than the record company they used to have wanted them to make a record. So I figured these guys were committed to doing it. And it sounded great: they had a lot of good songs and everyone was having fun.'

Press conferences were arranged, the usual bluster about this being the best album the quartet had ever recorded was quoted, and a tour was announced, before Graham Nash broke both his legs in a boating accident, and the album, *Looking Forward*, was released to lukewarm reviews. Inevitably, Young's contributions were singled out for special praise, while the other members were lambasted. Undeterred, the quartet announced the tour would go ahead in 2000, punningly dubbed Crosby, Stills, Nash & Young2K. At a press conference in Stockholm, Young enthused about playing guitar with Stills again, 35 years since they had first met in Fort William, Canada. 'You're my brother from another mother!' quipped Stills, good-naturedly.

After wending an often bizarre and tangential path over three and a half decades, Neil Young's career had, temporarily at least, come full circle.

TWO

THE MUSIC

All release dates are American, unless otherwise stated. On albums by Buffalo Springfield and Crosby, Stills, Nash & Young, only songs written or co-written by Neil Young are discussed. For compilations, only previously unreleased tracks are discussed.

Buffalo Springfield
Buffalo Springfield

Released:	January 1967
Chart position:	US: 80
	UK: —
Producers:	Brian Stone, Charles Greene
Engineers:	'Doc' Siegel, Tom May
Recorded:	July–October 1966, Gold Star Studios and Columbia Studios, both Los Angeles

Neil Young's long-playing debut was blighted by Buffalo Springfield managers Charles Greene and Brian Stone's appalling production. Their inexperience led to a thin, bass-free sound that robbed the band of their much-vaunted live power. Young's contributions shine through, both lyrically and melodically, certainly stronger than Stills's more numerous efforts, but overall this is far from classic stuff.

Baby Don't Scold Me
Go And Say Goodbye
Sit Down, I Think I Love You
Nowadays Clancy Can't Even Sing

Young's ode to childhood misery, sung by Richie Furay against a folk-rock backdrop that shifts neatly into waltz tempo on the chorus. Young and Stephen Stills provide harmonies.

Hot Dusty Roads
Everybody's Wrong
Flying On The Ground Is Wrong

Another Furay-sung Young composition and perhaps Young's best offering on the album. Clever, concise lyrics see lost love eulogised to an accompaniment of chiming guitars.

Burned

Young's snarling, effective vocal debut, robbed of its rock power by terrible production and trebly, badly-recorded guitars. A squandered opportunity, but he does play piano.

Do I Have To Come Right Out And Say It

Pleasant, if inconsequential, Byrds-y folk-rock ballad, sung by Furay, decorated with twelve-string guitars, lush harmonies and Young's barrel house piano.

Leave
Out Of My Mind

A Young-sung complaint about stardom's pressures, its doleful mood mirrored in a funereal rhythm even Furay and Stills's harmonies cannot lift.

Pay The Price

(note: 'Baby Don't Scold Me' was replaced by 'For What It's Worth' on pressings from February 1967)

Buffalo Springfield
Buffalo Springfield Again

Released: December 1967
Chart position: US: 44
UK: —
Producers: Brian Stone, Charles Greene, Richie Furay,
Stephen Stills, Neil Young, Ahmet Ertegun,
Jack Nitzsche
Engineers: Bruce Botnick, Jim Messina,
Ross Myering
Recorded: April–October 1967, studios including Gold Star,
Columbia, Sunset Sound and Sound Recorders,
Los Angeles and Atlantic Studios, New York

*With the band's three songwriters now working – and
occasionally recording – separately,* Buffalo Springfield
Again *boasts styles ranging from country and western
to Stonesy rock and swooning, string-laden pop, but has
little in the way of cohesion. Young's songwriting had
quickly become far more sophisticated and ambitious,
but as an album, this lurches too dramatically between
genres and ultimately is an unsatisfying experience.*

Mr Soul
Another broadside against the music industry, set to a driving, ferocious riff recalling The Rolling Stones' '(I Can't Get No) Satisfaction'.
Young's voice conveys bitterness, disgust and self-loathing in one
tortured warble.
A Child's Claim To Fame
Everydays
Expecting To Fly
Effectively a Young solo recording. Jack Nitzsche's melodramatic
strings back an exquisite tale of lost love: the melodic sweep into
the chorus is quite breathtaking.

Bluebird
Hung Upside Down
Sad Memory
Good Time Boy
Rock 'n' Roll Woman
Broken Arrow
   The ambition behind this post-*Sergeant Pepper* sound collage out-strips the disjointed result, but the fragile beauty of the constantly shifting rhythms is particularly affecting.

Buffalo Springfield
Last Time Around

Released:	August 1968
Chart Position:	US: 42
	UK: —
Producer:	Jim Messina
Engineer:	various
Recorded:	November 1967–May 1968, Sunset Sound, Los Angeles

Effectively compiled after the band's split by Richie Furay and sometime bassist Jim Messina, Last Time Around cannot be considered a 'proper' album. Bizarrely, however, it's more cohesive than its predecessor. It has a gently introspective mood, and, with the exception of perennial live favourite 'I Am A Child', Young's contributions are slight. By this stage, his best songs were saved for his solo career.

On The Way Home
   Horn-driven arrangement of a song regularly featured in Young's acoustic shows. Here, it sounds like a less malevolent version of fellow Los Angeles band Love.

It's So Hard To Wait

A soft-focus blues complete with jazz woodwind and brass arrangement. Rock critic Lester Bangs suggested the oblique lyric was about impotence.

Pretty Girl Why

Four Days Gone

Carefree Country Day

Special Care

The Hour Of Not Quite Rain

Questions

I Am A Child

Gentle country rhythms and *faux-naif* lyrics conspire to give an image of Young as wide-eyed, stoned innocence personified.

Merry-Go-Round

Uno Mundo

Kind Woman

Neil Young
Neil Young

Released:	November 1968
Chart Position:	US: —
	UK: —
Producers:	Dave Briggs, Neil Young, Jack Nitzsche, Ry Cooder
Engineers:	Mark Richardson, Donn Landee, Dale Batchelor, Rick Pekkonen, Henry Saskowski
Recorded:	June–October 1968, Sunwest Studios, Sunset Sound Recorders, Wally Heider Recording, California

'Overdub city,' commented Young some years after the release of his solo debut, and it's hard to argue with his assessment. It's not without its highlights, but the songs

*are of variable quality. The two instrumentals are hope-
lessly inconsequential, and virtually every track buckles
under the weight of Jack Nitzsche's overbearing orches-
trations and unnecessary production touches. Ry Cooder
helped out in the studio.*

The Emperor Of Wyoming
A surprisingly low-key start: an easy-on-the-ear country instrumental, jaunty without causing pulses to race.

The Loner
The first track recorded for the album, a strident, aggressive rocker,
marred by a faintly antiseptic, heavily overdubbed sound.

If I Could Have Her Tonight
Young the lovelorn dreamer returns to a jangling guitar accompaniment reminiscent of *Younger Than Yesterday*-era Byrds.

I've Been Waiting For You
Young's superb guitar solo (with modish stereo panning) is the highlight of this organ-based paean to idealised female perfection.

The Old Laughing Lady
A sinister death allegory which builds from hushed acoustic introduction, complete with subtle string arrangement, to soul-inspired
female chorus before a disturbing and protracted electric piano
fade.

String Quartet From Whiskey Boot Hill
Another brief instrumental, written by Jack Nitzsche, and presum-
ably part of an unfinished song: 'Whiskey Boot Hill' itself appears as
part of Crosby, Stills, Nash & Young's 'Country Girl' suite on *Déjà Vu*.

Here We Are In The Years
A beguiling melody married to ecologically concerned lyrics and a
beautifully restrained string arrangement make this an unqualified
success.

What Did You Do To My Life?
A puerile, accusatory lyric – 'I don't care…it isn't fair' – an unmemorable tune and a particularly childlike vocal from Young. Frankly, not
much fun.

I've Loved Her So Long

Another example of Young and Nitzsche's grandiose ambitions succeeding. Notably, the female backing singers and strings bolster rather than overpower Young's vocal.

The Last Trip To Tulsa

A messy, overlong acoustic ramble that strives – and fails – to achieve something approximate to Bob Dylan's 'Desolation Row' or 'Sad-Eyed Lady Of The Lowlands'.

Neil Young With Crazy Horse
Everybody Knows This Is Nowhere

Released:	May 1969
Chart Position:	US: 24
	UK: —
Producers:	David Briggs, Neil Young
Engineer:	David Briggs
Recorded:	20–29 March 1969, Sunset Sound, Hollywood

The album on which Young found an individual voice, with the cheerfully ramshackle help of Crazy Horse. Recorded quickly with the minimum of overdubbing, the album crackles with ferocious guitar playing and youthful energy. Far from outstaying their welcome, the two longest tracks are the highlights, although 'Cinnamon Girl' and the aching 'Round and Round (It Won't be Long)' proved that Young was equally adept at making his point concisely.

Cinnamon Girl

The concise Crazy Horse: nearly three minutes of crunching, open-tuned power chords, sparkling melodies and vocals that prize enthusiasm over finesse.

Everybody Knows This Is Nowhere
More off-key backing vocals as Young and Crazy Horse rubbish Los Angeles with distorted country-rock that embodies the album's aesthetic of laid-back thrills.

Round And Round (It Won't Be Long)
Magical vocals from Young, Whitten and Robin Lane over suitably hypnotic acoustic strumming gives this song a lulling beauty that transcends its fatalistic lyric.

Down By The River
Epic, troubled psychodrama: lengthy, stammering guitar solos build tension, the harmony-drenched chorus acts as release. It's over nine minutes long, but, oddly enough, none of it is superfluous.

The Losing End (When You're On)
The album's least distinguished track buries a clichéd lyric under a brazen country backing.

Running Dry (Requiem For The Rockets)
Grating violin and tremolo guitar add pathos and tension to this tale of oblique but intense regret. The title refers to Crazy Horse before Young renamed them.

Cowgirl In The Sand
The album's second ten-minute epic shares 'Down By the River''s structure of lengthy solos and explosive choruses, but replaces lyrical despair with lust.

Crosby, Stills, Nash & Young
Déjà Vu

Released:	March 1970
Chart Position:	US: 1
	UK: 5
Producers:	David Crosby, Stephen Stills, Graham Nash, Neil Young
Engineer:	Bill Halverson
Recorded:	11 June 1969–19 January 1970, Wally Heider

Recording, San Francisco

With the benefit of hindsight, Crosby, Stills, Nash & Young's debut sounds less the instant classic critics proclaimed on release, more an engaging period piece, complete with the benefits, flaws and excesses of its era. Nevertheless, Young's contributions were highlights, catching a transitional era between the three-part production extravaganza 'Country Girl' and the beautiful simplicity of 'Helpless'. The harmonies were, of course, exquisite.

Carry On
Teach Your Children
Almost Cut My Hair
Helpless
   Exquisite: Young's childhood memories set to three chords, endlessly repeated, with Crosby, Stills and Nash's typically soaring harmonies.
Woodstock
Deja Vu
Our House
4 + 20
Country Girl
   A three-part return to the epic balladry of 'Expecting To Fly', complete with 'Whiskey Boot Hill' and traces of 'Broken Arrow' about its beguiling melody.
Everybody I Love You
   Created by joining an unfinished Stills song to a riff by Young this is, harmonies aside, an unspectacular rocker that manages to meander despite its brevity.

Neil Young
After The Gold Rush

Released: September 1970
Chart Position: US: 8
UK: 7
Producers: Neil Young, David Briggs, with Kendall Pacios
Engineer: Kendall Pacios
Recorded: 2 August 1969–August 1970, Broken Arrow Studio, Redwood, California.

After The Gold Rush established the mercurial Young in a context the wider public could understand: as a purveyor of downbeat and troubled singer-songwriter fare. Despite such easy pigeonholing and an ever-shifting cast of sidemen, the album rarely puts a foot wrong, switching from stark ballads to guitar-heavy rock with deftness and ease. Some of Young's best-known and -loved material is here and Prelude did a lovely a cappella version of the title track, a hit twice over in Britain.

Tell Me Why
After The Gold Rush immediately sets out its musical store: simplistic songwriting and starkly recorded, darkly ponderous lyrics over a surprisingly jaunty musical backdrop.

After The Gold Rush
The wayward vocals add to the confused vulnerability of this science fiction eco-fable. Another minimal recording with piano joined by an uncredited, sombre French horn solo.

Only Love Can Break Your Heart
Melodically rich with a genuinely touching lyric, apparently aimed at Graham Nash. A stark acoustic arrangement highlights the glorious harmonies on the final verse.

Southern Man

Young's first expressly political track offers fierce guitar solos, a nagging riff and a harsh, distorted vocal that matches the lyrics' anti-racist anger. Lynyrd Skynyrd's 'Sweet Home Alabama' was written in response.

Till The Morning Comes

An idiosyncratic two-line fragment, which manages to cram in a jaunty French horn solo and some startling high harmonies.

Oh, Lonesome Me

An escapee from the aborted second Crazy Horse album, this maudlin Don Gibson cover finds both band and vocalist in decidedly shaky country-influenced form.

Don't Let It Bring You Down

Gloriously doom-laden, Young conjures up a series of disturbing images, while the unobtrusive and controlled musical backing matches 'Only Love Can Break Your Heart'.

Birds

One of Young's most effective and touching piano-led love songs. A blunt lyric – 'it's over' - masked by the loveliness of the melody and harmonies.

When You Dance You Can Really Love

A fine, fiery and surprisingly solo-free Young rocker that builds to a pounding climax, with driving, distorted guitar chords underpinned by a hammering piano.

I Believe In You

Another simple song which chronicles the demise of a relationship. As with 'Birds', the callousness of the lyric is obscured, this time by the positive title and chorus.

Cripple Creek Ferry

Another song fragment, this time a surprisingly cheerful singalong tale of the Old West, at odds with the general mood of the album, but charming nevertheless.

Crosby, Stills, Nash & Young
4 Way Street

Released:	February 1971
Chart Position:	US: 1
	UK: 5
Producers:	David Crosby, Stephen Stills, Graham Nash, Neil Young
Engineer:	Bill Halverson
Recorded (live):	June 2–7, Fillmore East, New York; June 26–28, Forum, Los Angeles; July 5 1970, Auditorium Theatre, Chicago

The bickering foursome live. The solo acoustic performances are variable. Young's self-deprecating simplicity presents a sharp contrast to Stills's pomposity, Crosby's simplicity and Nash's un-British naiveté. An extended 'Southern Man' and 'Ohio' are electric highlights, but overall this is a stopgap measure disguised (and accepted upon release) as a major statement. 'King Midas In Reverse', 'Laughing', 'Black Queen' and the Young medley were added to the 1992 reissued version, although they're contemporaneous with the original set list.

Suite: Judy Blue Eyes
On The Way Home
Teach Your Children
Triad
The Lee Shore
Chicago
Right Between The Eyes
Cowgirl In The Sand
Don't Let It Bring You Down
49 Bye Byes/America's Children
Love The One You're With

King Midas In Reverse
Laughing
Black Queen
Medley: The Loner/Cinnamon Girl/Down By The River
Pre-Road Downs
Long Time Gone
Southern Man
Ohio
Carry On
Find The Cost Of Freedom

Neil Young
Harvest

Released:	February 1972
Chart Position:	US: 1
	UK: 1
Producers:	Neil Young, Elliot Mazer, Jack Nitzsche, Henry Lewy
Engineer:	uncredited
Recorded:	February 1971–4 October 1971 at Quadrafonic Sound, Nashville; Broken Arrow Studio #2, California; Barking Town Hall, London; UCLA, California

Young's biggest-selling album was, in truth, a disappointment. Jack Nitzsche was back to ruin two tracks with his demolition-derby approach to orchestration, and, for the first time, Young appeared to be veering towards easy-listening and re-treading familiar ground: 'Alabama' was too close to 'Southern Man' for comfort. Harvest is at its best when at its most simple, but those moments are few and far between.

Out On The Weekend

A neat encapsulation of *Harvest*'s style (languorous, country-ish arrangements, polished production) and its failings (songwriting simplified to the point of banality).

Harvest

Repetitious simplicity, a gentle rhythm and restrained playing used to beguiling effect behind Young's lyric of courtly seduction. A highlight of an uneven album.

A Man Needs A Maid

The incongruous thundering of Jack Nitzsche and the London Symphony Orchestra during the chorus suggests this dubious celebration of domestic servitude takes itself far too seriously.

Heart Of Gold

Young's biggest-selling song is confident and assured, benefits from James Taylor and Linda Ronstadt's vocals, yet lacks the fiery conviction of Young at his best.

Are You Ready For The Country

Some thrilling pedal steel guitar from Ben Keith – leader of Young's latest band Stray Gators – aside, this is a lacklustre performance, rambling, inconsequential and quite at odds with the challenge of its title. Crosby and Nash help out on backing vocals.

Old Man

Harvest's other standout. Excellent banjo playing and steel guitar woven around a reflective lyric, inspired by Young's ranch-hand Louis Avila. It reached Number 31 in the American singles chart.

There's A World

Another outing for Nitzsche and the London Symphony Orchestra, and it's no less bombastic than the first. Portentous, pretentious and overwrought with kettle drums and tasteless harps.

Alabama

'Southern Man', with additional Crosby and Stills vocals and *Harvest*'s most intense guitar playing. It does, however, successfully build a mood of brooding anger.

The Needle And The Damage Done

One of Young's most celebrated songs, a plaintive acoustic lament inspired by Crazy Horse guitarist Danny Whitten's first, non-fatal heroin overdose. Recorded live at UCLA.

Words (Between The Lines Of Age)

An intense performance, marred slightly by a dragging pace, 'Words' nevertheless ends *Harvest* on an epic note far more convincing than the album's orchestral experiments.

Journey Through The Past
Original Soundtrack Recording

Released:	November 1972
Chart Position:	US: 45
	UK: —
Producer/ Engineer:	various
Compiled by	Neil Young
Recorded:	various live tracks and rehearsals between February 1967 and 1971

A rag-bag of decidedly mixed live performances – the side-long version of 'Words' is interminable – alongside an old Beach Boys track, choral music and one new Young tune, the 1970 piano ballad 'Soldier'. As inexplicable as the film it soundtracked, Journey Through The Past *sounds hurriedly thrown together and disjointed.*

For What It's Worth
Mr. Soul
Rock And Roll Woman
  (all Buffalo Springfield live tracks)
Find The Cost Of Freedom
Ohio
Southern Man
  (all Crosby, Stills, Nash & Young live tracks)

Are You Ready For The Country?
   (Neil Young)
Let Me Call You Sweetheart
   (uncredited girls' chorus)
Alabama
Words
   (both Neil Young)
Relativity Invitation
   (dialogue from the film)
Handel's Messiah
King Of Kings
   (both Tony & Susan Alamo Christian Foundation Orchestra & Chorus)
Soldier
   (Neil Young)
Let's Go Away For A While
   (The Beach Boys)

Neil Young
Time Fades Away

Released:	September 1973
Chart Position:	US: 22
	UK: 20
Producers:	Neil Young, Elliot Mazer
Engineer:	uncredited
Recorded (live):	11 February–29 March 1973 at Oklahoma City
	Myriad, Cleveland Public Hall, Seattle Coliseum,
	UCLA Royce Hall, Phoenix Coliseum, Sacramento
	Memorial Auditorium, San Diego Sports Arena

The opposite of Harvest's *over-produced MOR gloss.*
Time Fades Away *is live, muffled, wildly discordant, sloppily played and chilling, compelling listening. What it lacked*

in finesse was compensated for by Young's raw emotional power. As a document of a tormented man disillusioned by the fallout of the 1960s, it remains quite astonishing.

Time Fades Away

The path to *Tonight's The Night* signposted: heroin lyrics, pounding piano, wildly thrashing drums and chaotic vocals. Grating, chilling, but disturbingly effective.

Journey Through The Past

A lovely piano ballad that could have fitted on *After The Gold Rush* were it not for its rough playing, occasional bum notes and wracked vocal.

Yonder Stands The Sinner

Loose even by these standards. Young's raw-throated vocal is miles out, the band plays bluesy rock out of tune, Crosby and Nash are inaudible.

L.A.

Its melody a sickly cousin of 'Cinnamon Girl', 'L.A.' praises and demonises Los Angeles. Rolling piano and fluid guitar make for one of this strange album's most enjoyable moments.

Love In Mind

A melody sweet enough for *Harvest* fuels this short, touching ballad, delivered solo at the piano.

Don't Be Denied

An anthem deliberately undersold by its grinding performance. It offers Young's biography and personal philosophy alongside some powerful slide guitar.

The Bridge

A rare ray of light among the darkness, a simple affirmation of the healing power of love.

Last Dance

Young's first attempt to bury the Woodstock myth, underpinned by a band gradually falling apart as the song's dark riff churns endlessly on.

Neil Young
On The Beach

Released: July 1974
Chart Position: US: 16
UK: 42
Producers: Neil Young, David Briggs, Mark Harman, Al Schmitt
Engineer: uncredited
Recorded: March–April 1974, Sunset Sound, Los Angeles;
Broken Arrow, San Francisco

An overlooked classic in the Young oeuvre, On The Beach's relentless misery was hopelessly out of step with prevalent trends on its release. The playing on the album – sidemen included The Band's Rick Danko and Levon Helm – is exemplary, even funky: a first for Young. Its gleeful dissection of the failed hippie dream is spot-on, and Young has rarely sounded as blackly humorous as on the disturbing 'Revolution Blues'.

Walk On
The album's solitary uplifting moment, a reaction to criticism of the then-unreleased *Tonight's The Night*, with a surprisingly funky rhythm and a strange, deep vocal.
See The Sky About To Rain
Dating from Young's 1971 acoustic shows and covered by The Byrds, this gentle, electric piano-led track is subdued by comparison with the rest of *On The Beach*.
Revolution Blues
One of Young's finest songs, an awesomely powerful, darkly humorous satire of 1960s values, driven along by Crosby's rhythm guitar and The Band's rhythm section.
For The Turnstiles
The fleeting fame of baseball celebrity examined while clattering percussion, banjo, dobro and what sounds like someone stamping

on the floor create a backwoods, rootsy feel.

Vampire Blues

A rather plodding, blues-influenced attack on oil companies, which fits with *On The Beach*'s downcast mood, but is overshadowed by its illustrious neighbours.

On The Beach

Lazy bongos and rhythm guitar contrast with a precise solo, reflecting the confused cost-of-fame lyrics ('I need a crowd of people but I can't face them every day').

Motion Pictures

Written in a hotel room, 'Motion Pictures' undercuts its twin analyses of touring and Young's current relationship with a stoned, lethargic melancholy.

Ambulance Blues

Young constructs a surreal, beautifully-sung Dylanesque monologue, while his harmonica and Rusty Kershaw's fiddle interlock to considerable effect.

Neil Young
Tonight's The Night

Released:	June 1975
Chart Position:	US: 25
	UK: 48
Producer:	David Briggs, Neil Young with Tim Mulligan; Elliot Mazer
Engineer:	Gabby Garcia, Tim Mulligan
Recorded:	7 March 1970, Fillmore East, New York; 20 August–12 September 1973 and 18 October 1974, Broken Arrow, San Francisco; Studio Instrument Rentals Rehearsal Hall "D", Hollywood

A remarkable exercise in method acting. Young and his band (now led by Nils Lofgren) are audibly smashed, his voice cracks and jars throughout, the playing is sketchy, but Tonight's The Night *remains perhaps Young's most powerful album, at turns funny, beautiful, cacophonous and desperately sad. A fitting epitaph to friends felled by heroin, its mood encapsulated in 'Tired Eyes'' refrain: 'He tried to do his best, but he could not'.*

Tonight's The Night
Guitar roadie Bruce Berry agonisingly eulogised: the backing is shambolic and strangely muted, leaving Young's voice – equal parts grief, anger and tequila – vulnerable and exposed.

Speakin' Out
Utterly ravaged blues, complete with tipsy honky-tonk piano. Lofgren's solo is slickly played, but the aura of woozy, early-hours melancholy remains paramount.

World On A String
Sprightly by comparison with much of the album, this still maintains the feel of a shambolic jam, complete with chaotic, jumbled backing vocals.

Borrowed Tune
A stark solo piano number, its melody stolen from The Rolling Stones' 'Lady Jane', compounding the lyrical theme of confusion and self-doubt. Wholly solo.

Come On Baby Let's Go Downtown
Live at New York's Fillmore East, co-writer Danny Whitten sings of scoring heroin at a 1970 Crazy Horse gig. A thrilling, tight performance, a poignant aural and emotional counterpoint.

Mellow My Mind
Another bravura vocal performance from an audibly sozzled Young, a tale of post-tour madness reflected in his failure to reach the high notes.

Roll Another Number (For The Road)
A drunken, sneering satire on the Woodstock nation, its ungainly country swing, fumbling playing and slurred vocal simply adds to its nihilistic, pre-punk appeal.

Albuquerque

In tune for the first time on the album, Young yearns for anonymity over one of *Tonight's The Night*'s most straightforward (and sober) performances.

New Mama

In the midst of an album laden with death, a brief respite came via this touching celebration of motherhood delivered in the close harmony style of Crosby, Stills, Nash & Young.

Lookout Joe

A *Time Fades Away* outtake, which accounts for its dense guitar sound, warning soldiers returning from Vietnam that America is awash with drugs and misery.

Tired Eyes

Young relates the (apparently true) story of a cocaine deal gone murderously wrong in a disturbingly matter-of-fact voice over a slow country backing.

Tonight's The Night (Part II)

The album closes on a bleak note. This version of 'Tonight's The Night' is even more ragged than the first, full of wrong notes, fluffed vocals and palpable drunken tension.

Neil Young With Crazy Horse
Zuma

Released:	November 1975
Chart Position:	US: 25
	UK: 44
Producers:	Neil Young, David Briggs, Tim Mulligan
Engineer:	George Horn
Recorded:	3–12 July, 1975

A return to the straightforward rocking values of Everybody Knows This Is Nowhere. *The guitar playing on* Zuma *is luminous, the songs exemplary.* Crazy Horse *charge though boozy anthems such as 'Barstool Blues' and play with elegiac subtlety on 'Cortez The Killer'. And the Crosby, Stills, Nash & Young closer, 'Through My Sails', remains the strongest extant argument for the quartet's continued existence.*

Don't Cry No Tears
The confident fire of 'Cinnamon Girl' recaptured by Crazy Horse on one of Young's earliest songs, its theme a refutation of the three albums which preceded *Zuma*.

Danger Bird
A slow-burning performance of brooding, epic intensity. Some of Young's guitar work is extraordinary.

Pardon My Heart
Crazy Horse's doo-wop roots are audible in the backing vocals of this ballad. Curiously, the guitar solo is mixed lower than the acoustic guitars.

Lookin' For A Love
Zuma's most commercial moment, although the demons of the last three years are still present in Young's lyrical reference to 'the darker side of me'.

Barstool Blues
Crazy Horse at their most concise and glorious, their cocksure swagger undercut by the hint of desperation in Young's vocal, mixed high, and the troubled final verse.

Stupid Girl
A vicious character assassination – allegedly directed at Joni Mitchell – set to a relaxed Crazy Horse backing, the weakest track here by some distance.

Drive Back
Another straightforward rocker – a mode virtually absent from Young's work since 1969 – more a vehicle for striking soloing than a memorable song.

Cortez The Killer
A remarkable centerpiece, its guitar playing and storytelling are

equally spellbinding. Despite the loss of one verse as a result of a studio power failure, this is close to perfection.

Through My Sails
Dispensing with Crazy Horse at the death, this gentle lullaby features Crosby, Stills & Nash. It's as beautiful in its harmony-laden simplicity – acoustic guitar, bass and congas – as anything they recorded.

The Stills-Young Band
Long May You Run

Released:	October 1976
Chart Position:	US: 26
	UK: 12
Producers:	Stephen Stills, Neil Young, Don Gehman
Engineers:	Michael Lasko, Steve Hart
Recorded:	April 1976, Criteria Studios, Miami

With the exception of the nostalgic title track, this was another disaster. Long May You Run has a charmless, antiseptic production – possibly the result of Stills's nit-picking quest for sonic perfection – but Young's songs, as bland as anything he's committed to vinyl, hardly help matters. Hardly worth falling out with Nash and Crosby for.

Long May You Run
The one substantial Young track here, a touching inversion of the traditional California car song, with a neat reference to The Beach Boys' equally romantic 'Caroline, No'.

Make Love To You
Midnight On The Bay
A slight song, propped up by glossy production, this is virtually the epitome of bland mid-'70s rock. Remarkable only in that Neil Young

Left A long way from Crazy Horse: a betassled Young on stage with Buffalo Springfield.

Right Another shot that Young probably wishes had never seen the light of day: Buffalo Springfield ham it up Monkee-style, c. 1967.

Above From left: Graham Nash, David Crosby, and Neil Young in harmony on stage, at least.

Below A more casual Young, still haunted by a tassel fetish at the time of the release of *Déjà Vu, c.*1970.

Neil Young the solo artist, in typically energetic onstage form.

Above With Crazy Horse (from left: Frank Sampedro, Ralph Molina, Neil Young, Billy Talbot).

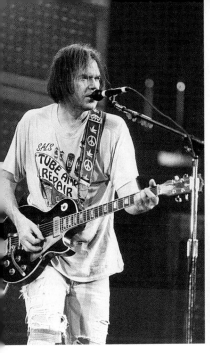

Left, above and right The many
faces of Neil Young in performance:
in 'Cinnamon Girl' (left below), 'Like
A Hurricane' (above) and 'Godfather
of Grunge' mode (right below).

Above From Devo to Willie Nelson, Young's influence remains almost impossible to categorise. Here seen with Nelson at Farm Aid, 1985.
Below In the 1990s, Young provided inspiration for a new generation of musicians, including grunge icons Kurt Cobain and Eddie Vedder.

Above and right
Young continues to be a supporter of Farm Aid. Here seen meeting the press at the event in 1985, above, and again in 1994, right.

1999's long-awaited reunion of Crosby, Stills, Nash and Young proved both a commercial and critical disappointment but, once again, it was Young who was singled out for what praise there was. Left to right: Neil Young, Graham Nash, David Crosby and Stephen Stills.

could make something so unadventurous.

Black Coral

Ocean Girl

Wah-wah guitar, a reggae-influenced beat and massed harmonies fail to lift this relaxed but banal string of ethnic clichés.

Let It Shine

Thrashy guitar, wayward harmonies and a confused search for spiritual redemption in the lyrics, all rendered antiseptic and unimpressive by over-production.

12/8 Blues (All The Same)

Fontainebleau

Despite some intriguing soloing from Young and a lyric that spits bile at a Miami hotel (of all things) this is essentially as unmemorable as the rest of *Long May You Run*.

Guardian Angel

Neil Young
American Stars 'n' Bars

Released:	June 1977
Chart Position:	US: 21
	UK: 17
Producers:	Neil Young, David Briggs, Tim Mulligan, Elliot Mazer
Engineer:	uncredited
Recorded:	November 1974, November 1975, May 1976 and April 1977 at Broken Arrow, Redwood, California.

It's difficult to know what Young was attempting to achieve with this bewildering collection of rush-recorded country tunes, lo-fi acoustic outtakes and blazing Crazy Horse tracks, but whatever it was, he failed. A curate's egg means a couple of highlights – 'Like A Hurricane' and the unsettling 'Will To Love' – are outnumbered by lumpy, unlovable filler.

The Old Country Waltz
Boozy melancholy, but less angsty and effective than 'Tonight's The Night'. Woozy fiddle and pedal steel back Young, Linda Ronstadt and Nicolette Larson's vocals.

Saddle Up the Palomino
Crazy Horse serve up a leaden, noisy backing for this lyrically witty but ultimately unengaging tale of adulterous intent.

Hey Babe
One of the strongest melodies on the album, but the lyrics are appalling. The jaunty, roughly-played backing – pedal steel to the fore – has some charm.

Hold Back The Tears
Another unmemorable country excursion, with Young's vocal swamped by Larson and Ronstadt. Once again, the lyrics are feeble, offering dull platitudes of positivity.

Bite The Bullet
A lumpy and unconvincing rocker complete with ghastly, sexually-charged lyrics and Ronstadt and Larson wailing away in risible 1970s rock-chick style.

Star Of Bethlehem
Emmylou Harris guests, adding rich harmonies to this short and largely unspectacular country-influenced examination of the failings of love.

Will To Love
Recorded entirely solo by Young, this is *American Stars 'n' Bars*'s obvious standout track, a melange of muffled acoustic guitar, strange percussion and soft vocals.

Like A Hurricane
This is among Young's most famous songs, but the version here – a pedestrian reading that only catches fire towards the end of Young's solo – is hardly definitive.

Homegrown
Like an electric 'Cripple Creek Ferry', this ends the album on a low-key note with a tubthumping, amusing squib, packed with marijuana double-entendres.

Neil Young
Decade

Released:	November 1977
Chart Position:	US: 48
	UK: 46
Producer:	various
Compiled:	Neil Young, Tim Mulligan, David Briggs
Engineer:	various
Recorded:	various

> *An fairly impeccable collection of greatest hits and unre-leased material.* On The Beach, Time Fades Away *and* Tonight's The Night *are all deliberately under-repre-sented, which gives sonic consistency at the expense of brutal emotional power, but* Decade *still stands as a fine introduction to Young's '60s and '70s work. It also nobly upheld Young's sometime tradition of illegible sleevenotes, started on* Neil Young *itself.*

Buffalo Springfield: Down To The Wire
Buffalo Springfield at their best: a reverb-drenched tale of obsessive love, complete with massed Stills harmonies, backwards guitar and piano from Dr John. From the unreleased *Stampede* album.
Burned
Young's first ever vocal (1966).
Mr. Soul
Broken Arrow
Expecting to Fly
I Am A Child
Crosby Stills, Nash & Young: Helpless
Ohio
Recorded and mixed at lightning speed, this is the quartet's most convincing political statement, the anger and indignation still fresh in the guitar breaks and vocals.

The Stills-Young Band: Long May You Run
Solo and with Stray Gators or Crazy Horse
Sugar Mountain
A perennial live favourite, a simple acoustic lament recorded on a home tape recorder that makes up in heartfelt emotion what it loses in clunking lyrical couplets.
The Loner
The Old Laughing Lady
Cinnamon Girl
Down By The River
Cowgirl In The Sand
I Believe In You
After The Gold Rush
Southern Man
Soldier
Old Man
A Man Needs A Maid
Harvest
Heart Of Gold
Star Of Bethlehem
The Needle And The Damage Done
Tonight's The Night (Part 1)
Tired Eyes
Walk On
For The Turnstiles
Winterlong
A strong *On The Beach* outtake, 'Winterlong' shares that album's combination of full band sound, strong melodic sense and lyrical and vocal despair.
Deep Forbidden Lake
Written, in 1975, to signal the end of Young's 'dark period', this is an appealing simple tune complete with fiddle solo, celebrating the joys of nature.
Like A Hurricane
Love Is A Rose

Recorded during Crosby, Stills, Nash & Young's aborted 1974 session in Hawaii, this two-minute song sounds unfinished, but stamped percussion and country picking lend a rustic appeal. Linda Ronstadt covered it.

Cortez The Killer

Campaigner

The finest of *Decade*'s 'new' tracks, a moving, mature examination of human grief. The sudden loss of reverb in the fade-out completes the song's intimacy. Written on The Stills-Young Band's tour bus.

Neil Young
Comes A Time

Released:	November 1978
Chart Position:	US: 7
	UK: 42
Producers:	Neil Young, Ben Keith, Tim Mulligan, David Briggs
Engineers:	Tim Mulligan, Michael Laskow, David McKinley, Danny Hilly, Mike Porter, Denny Purcell, Rich "Hoss" Adler, Ernie Winfrey, Gabby Garcia, Paul Kaminsky
Recorded:	October-December 1977 at Triiad, Fort Lauderdale; Columbia, London; Wally Heider, Hollywood; Woodland, Nashville; Sound Shop, Nashville; Broken Arrow, Redwood, California.

The studio gloss of Harvest *returns, but this time the songs are considerably stronger, boosted by Nicolette Larson's excellent vocals and over 30 Nashville sessionmen. The string arrangements are unintrusive, Crazy Horse's two contributions are excellent, and, the ghastly aberration of 'Motorcycle Mama' aside, this is Young's softer side at its best.*

Goin' Back

Sets out the album's store both lyrically (a return to old values) and musically (Larson's vocals, massed acoustic guitars, polished production, subtle orchestration).

Comes A Time

More lyrical homilies — 'this ol' world keeps turnin' round' — beautifully orchestrated, with a fine Larson vocal and sparsely effective drumming.

Look Out For My Love

The first of Crazy Horse's two contributions offers rougher, more dynamic playing, a particularly mournful Young vocal and final verses spiked with trademark feedback.

Lotta Love

Melodically luscious, Crazy Horse's tough playing — including some surprisingly driving drums — prevent the song from becoming overly saccharine.

Peace Of Mind

A song that rambles musically and lyrically, with its portentous military drumming and an arrangement that relies on an awkward muddle of strings and pedal steel.

Human Highway

Another leftover from the 1974 Crosby, Stills, Nash & Young sessions, this re-recording highlights a slight song elevated by bubbling banjo picking and beautifully understated slide guitar.

Already One

Young dissects his failed relationship with Carrie Snodgrass for the umpteenth time, but if the melody and arrangement are slightly flat, the lyrics are poignant and moving.

Field Of Opportunity

A slyly cynical assessment of the album's commercial potential — 'in the field of opportunity, it's ploughing time again' — with some sprightly country fiddle.

Motorcycle Mama

A turgid, lifeless rocker, complete with Larson wailing away, this is a dramatic lapse of taste on an album prized for its tastefulness.

Four Strong Winds

Ian & Sylvia's 1963 Canadian folk standard, thickly coated with 12-string guitars, veering towards MOR, but still the album's most commercial moment.

Neil Young & Crazy Horse
Rust Never Sleeps

Released: June 1979
Chart Position: US: 8
UK: 13
Producers: Neil Young, David Briggs, Tim Mulligan
Engineer: uncredited
Recorded: May 1978-January 1979 at The Boarding House, San Francisco; McNicholl's Arena, Denver; Civic Center Arena, St. Paul; Cow Palace, San Francisco; Broken Arrow, Redwood, California.

Half-acoustic, half-electric, partially live, partially studio-bound, Rust Never Sleeps *was Young's thrilling response to punk. Lyrically sharp (check the stinging 'Thrasher' for proof), melodically inspired, and intense without becoming overbearing, the album was as close to perfection as an artist as eclectic as Young is ever going to get.*

My My, Hey Hey (Out Of The Blue)

After the slick commerciality of *Comes A Time*, this places Young at the centre of the new wave, comparing Johnny Rotten to Elvis on a solo acoustic performance.

Thrasher

12-string acoustic guitar backs Young's thrillingly barbed assessment of his career, poking a satirical finger at Crosby, Stills & Nash in the process.

Ride My Llama

A jokey throwaway left over from *Zuma*, this tune about a dope-smoking alien is a slight, but amusing diversion from the previous tracks' philosophising.

Pocahontas

Percussive acoustic guitar-playing and Beach-Boys-influenced backing vocals add to a weighty, affecting lyric which offers belated solidarity with Native Americans. They must have been delighted.

Sail Away

A smoothly-produced *Comes A Time* outtake, 'Sail Away' is musically incongruous here, but its lyrics about fame fit neatly among *Rust Never Sleeps's* other themes.

Powderfinger

The point where Crazy Horse actually join us, despite the album's credit. An epic Young narrative (the lyrics are brilliantly executed), a wonderful main riff and Crazy Horse's restrained playing make this one of Young's finest moments.

Welfare Mothers

A token error of judgement, a club-footed rocker with offensive lyrics about the sexual prowess of poverty-stricken divorcees. Even Young's ferocious soloing can't save it.

Sedan Delivery

Clearly influenced by punk in its shifts from frantically thrashed garage band riffs to languid, half-speed feedback sprawl. Lyrically confused but thoroughly exciting.

My My, Hey Hey (Into The Black)

An impossibly distorted take on the album opener, this features a guitar sound for which the adjective 'grunge' could have been (and possibly was) invented for.

Neil Young & Crazy Horse
Live Rust

Released: November 1979
Chart Position: US: 15

UK: 55

Producers: David Briggs, Tim Mulligan, Bernard Shakey (aka
Young and Dean Stockwell)
Engineer: David Hewitt
Recorded: September–October 1978 at various shows during
the *Rust Never Sleeps* tour.

*Vilified as an unnecessary cash-in on release, a few
months after the partially-live* Rust Never Sleeps, Live
Rust *stands up well 20 years later. The performances
are tight and powerful, the selection of material well
thought out and, as a document of Crazy Horse at a live
peak, it works perfectly. That said, it's not an essential
purchase – there are no unreleased songs among its
tracks – and it's not without artistic flaws: Young's decision to sing the coda of 'Cortez The Killer' in a cod-
Jamaican accent is a questionable judgement at best.*

Sugar Mountain
I Am A Child
Comes A Time
After The Gold Rush
My My, Hey Hey (Out Of The Blue)
When You Dance I Can Really Love
The Loner
The Needle And The Damage Done
Lotta Love
Sedan Delivery
Powderfinger
Cortez The Killer
Cinnamon Girl
Like A Hurricane
Hey Hey, My My (Into The Black)
Tonight's The Night

Neil Young
Hawks And Doves

Released: October 1980
Chart Position: US: 30
UK: 34
Producers: David Briggs, Tim Mulligan, Neil Young
Engineer: Elliot Mazer, Michael Laskow, Paul Kaminisky, Richard Kaplan, Jerry Napier
Recorded: June 1980, Village Studios, Los Angeles; Quadrafonic Sound Studio, Nashville; Triad Recording Studios, Fort Lauderdale; Indigo Ranch Studio, Malibu; Gold Star Recording Studios, Hollywood

Distracted by family strife, Young effectively compiled American Stars 'n' Bars II: another muddled collection of country tunes and other offcuts, seemingly compiled at random. The best moments are pleasant enough – 'Little Wing''s acoustic simplicity, for instance – but at their worst, as on 'Union Man', the low points are very low indeed.

Little Wing
The downbeat mood of the album is set with this brief acoustic track, featuring some striking, close-miked harmonica and gently affecting, if oblique, lyrics.

The Old Homestead
'Why do you ride that Crazy Horse?' asks Young sardonically on this lengthy but stark extended allegory for his own mercurial career.

Lost In Space
Another solo performance, a beautiful melody with utterly unintelligible lyrics – 'don't draw on the infinity board' – marred by irritating sped-up backing vocals.

Captain Kennedy
First recorded for the unreleased *Chrome Dreams* album in 1976, this low-key country track boasts yet another curiously oblique lyric,

but its simplicity holds a sinister power.

Stayin' Power

A return to the cod-country of *American Stars 'n' Bars*, saved only by its lyric, an impassioned tribute to Young's seemingly ailing wife, Pegi.

Coastline

An unappealing mix of rockabilly and hokey country and western backs another touching lyric depicting the strength of the Youngs' marriage in adversity.

Union Man

A satirical dig at the Musicians Union, which chuckles 'Live Music Is Better, bumper stickers should be issued!'. Amusing, but not quite enough to distract attention from the limp country backing.

Comin' Apart At Every Nail

Confusingly, melodically similar to 'Union Man', this features strong vocals from Ann Hillary O'Brien, but the song itself is unmemorable.

Hawks And Doves

Bewildering political satire, delivered in a preposterously affected Southern accent. Its flag-waving would seem less amusing in the light of Young's later pro-Reagan remarks.

Neil Young & Crazy Horse
Re-Ac-Tor

Released: October 1981
Chart Position: US: 27
UK: 69
Producer: Neil Young, David Briggs, Tim Mulligan
Engineer: uncredited
Recorded: October–December 1980, Broken Arrow, Redwood, California.

Crazy Horse tried to inject a spark of excitement into the half-formed jams and thumpingly dull rock tracks that made up Re-Ac-Tor, *but they fought a losing battle against Young's disinterest. His mind was on his handicapped son's condition, and for the first time in his solo career, Young sounded as if he didn't really care. The anguished closer 'Shots' demonstrated what might have been.*

Opera Star

A self-deprecating look at rock star life, set to a bone-crunching Crazy Horse riff, embellished with synthesizers and ruined by appalling falsetto backing vocals.

Surfer Joe And The Sleaze

The best tune on an album hardly overburdened with melody, it once again suffers from heavy-handed backing vocals and a curiously disinterested Young vocal.

T-Bone

Re-Ac-Tor's repetitive aesthetic *in extremis*: two lines of lyrics repeated for 10 minutes. Less a song than an endurance test, subsequently and sensibly (although they might have mentioned their unease at the time) disowned by Crazy Horse.

Get Back On It

A limp pastiche of 1950s rock 'n' roll, lifelessly performed, poorly mixed – the drums are virtually inaudible – and lyrically tedious.

Southern Pacific

Rhythmically influenced by the train of its title, this chugs along unremarkably, and stands out on *Re-ac-tor* only by dint of it having some semblance of a tune.

Motor City

An annoyingly banal affair; lyrics that revive the jingoism of *Hawks And Doves* ('there's far too many Datsuns in this town'), uninspired playing. A nadir of sorts.

Rapid Transit

Young makes idiotic gurgling car noises over an implausibly simple riff. An acerbic guitar solo aside, 'Rapid Transit' has little to recommend it.

Shots

The album's one truly great moment: eight minutes of impassioned vocals, guitars distorted to cacophony, explosive soloing and a thrilling feedback finale.

Neil Young
Trans

Released:	December 1982
Chart Position:	US: 19
	UK: 29
Producers:	Neil Young, David Briggs, Tim Mulligan
Engineer:	uncredited
Recorded:	May–July 1982, Modern Recorders, Redwood, California; Commercial Recorders, Honolulu

Full marks for trying to do something new with synthesizers, but good intentions don't necessarily make a good album. The 'concept' behind the songs is flawed, the inclusion of straightforward guitar-based tracks makes the vocoders and synthesizers sound gimmicky and, perversely, Trans now sounds far more dated than, say, Everybody Knows This Is Nowhere.

Little Thing Called Love

An anaemic rocker left over from the rejected *Island In The Sun* album. It kicks off the album in traditional, if underwhelming style, with no clue of what is to follow.

Computer Age

The strongest of the synthesizer experiments offers a meaty riff and a re-write of Kraftwerk's 'Computer World'. The vocoder is teeth-gritting and horribly dated.

We R In Control

More echoes of Kraftwerk as Young attempts to marry Crazy

Horse-like riffing with then-contemporary technology, to little effect.

Transformer Man

Young's ode to his mentally handicapped son boasts one of *Trans's* strongest melodies, but the vocodered vocal renders it virtually unlistenable.

Computer Cowboy (AKA Syscrusher)

Another attempt to match swampy riffing with vocodered vocals and mechanical rhythms. By now, the novelty is starting to wear gossamer-thin.

Hold On To Your Love

Mercifully vocoder-free, this track sounds like a thinly produced outtake from *Comes A Time,* with ill-fitting synthesizers attached apropos of nothing.

Sample And Hold

More plodding rhythms and unintelligible vocodered vocals, with no discernible tune – or fun – whatsoever.

Mr. Soul

An interesting idea that falls flat, this electronic remake of the Buffalo Springfield tune succeeds in removing every ounce of funk, anger and sass from the original. Well done, Neil.

Like An Inca

Tucked away at the album's end is a fine, harmony-laden extended guitar workout, complete with some muscular soloing. Again thinly produced, it's still the best thing here.

Neil Young & The Shocking Pinks
Everybody's Rockin'

Released:	August 1983
Chart Position:	US: 46
	UK: 50
Producers:	Neil Young, Elliot Mazer
Engineers:	Tim Mulligan, John Nowland, Mike Herbick

Recorded: March 1983, Modern Recorders, Redwood, California.

It probably sounded like a good idea live, but in the studio, Young's rockabilly pastiches fall flat. His voice is ill-suited to such material, the digital production robs the album of the warm sound of real 1950s recordings, the covers are ill-chosen and the originals are deadly dull. And, at 24 minutes long, it's a rip-off as well.

Betty Lou's Got A New Pair Of Shoes
A limp cover of a Bobby Freeman track makes for an inauspicious start, with Ben King's saxophone break the only real saving grace.

Rainin' In My Heart
The performance here is overshadowed by Young's terrible, misguided attempt at a spoken section, a toe-curling embarrassment not easily forgotten.

Payola Blues
A hint of classic anti-music-business Young peeks through on this song comparing the payola scandal surrounding 1950s DJ Alan Freed with the modern-day industry.

Wonderin'
That Geffen released this inoffensive doo-wop track as a single is less an indication of its quality than of how desperate Young's label had become by 1983. It's hard not to sympathise with The Man.

Kinda Fonda Wanda
At least Young sounds like he's having fun on this Jerry Lee Lewis pastiche. In fact, it seems likely Young had more fun than those who had to listen to the finished product.

Jellyroll Man
Another rockabilly pastiche – complete with skull-numbingly awful harmonica solo – that probably sounded like great fun on stage, but is simply not strong enough to bear repeated home listening.

Bright Lights, Big City
A genuinely dreadful cover of Jimmy Reed's R&B classic: any number

of pick-up bar bands around the world could have performed this with an equal lack of conviction.

Mystery Train

Another unconvincing cover, this time of Elvis Presley's classic 1955 Sun single.

Cry, Cry, Cry

A Young original in the doo-wop mode, 'Cry, Cry, Cry' drags along, appearing to last far longer than its listed two and a half minutes.

Everybody's Rockin'

Another weak Young original with terrible lyrics about 'Nancy and Ronnie' rocking in the White House rounds off a singularly unimpressive album.

Neil Young
Old Ways

Released:	August 1985
Chart Position:	US: 75
	UK: 39
Producers:	Neil Young, Ben Keith, David Briggs
Engineer:	Gene Eichelberger
Recorded:	April 1985, The Castle, Franklin, Tennessee

Young was perfectly capable of making good country music – see Comes A Time *for proof – but this exercise in Nashville schlock did neither artist nor genre any favours. The arrangements pile on the syrup and the songwriting is lost in a mire of clichés that leave the album sounding more parody than the results of a heartfelt interest in the genre.*

The Wayward Wind

Swirling strings and syrupy vocals from Denise Draper on a song too slight to merit such an overdone production: it sets the parody tone with bewildering gusto.

Get Back To The Country

Introduces a Jew's harp into the proceedings in a misguided attempt to jolly along a mass of lyrical clichés and uninspired songwriting.

Are There Any More Real Cowboys?

Young casts a characteristically jaded eye over Nashville with guest vocalist Willie Nelson. Mercifully free of orchestras, it remains a rare highlight of *Old Ways*.

Once An Angel

A mawkish and clichéd love song. As an embellishment, the massed female choir ranks alongside 'Get Back To The Country' 's Jew's harp.

Misfits

A preposterous lyric about space travel and 'see-through hookers' suffering sneezing fits. Waylon Jennings duets, while the swirling strings are much in evidence again.

California Sunset

Fiddler Rufus Thibodeaux tries his best, but all the dextrous technique in the world can't help this instantly forgettable tune.

Old Ways

'Old ways can be a ball and chain,' sings Young in cheeky refutation of his past, but once again, the song sounds like a lifeless parody, this time of a Southern boogie.

My Boy

The album's one truly great song, as the author of 'Old Man' finds himself facing middle age to a stately, controlled backing of banjo and pedal steel.

Bound For Glory

Another weak melody (and appalling lyrics about an adulterous trucker romancing a hitch-hiker) stretched out over five minutes.

Where Is The Highway Tonight?

Melodically appealing and boasting another guest vocal from Waylon Jennings, this closes a desperately uneven album on a relatively positive note.

Neil Young
Landing On Water

Released: July 1986
Chart Position: US: 46
UK: 52
Producers: Neil Young, Danny Kortchmar
Engineers: Niko Bolas, Tim Mulligan
Recorded: Record One, Los Angeles

Young's songs were ill-suited to the sample-heavy, mid-'80s production of Landing On Water. *His voice and guitar are marooned over clanking robotic rhythm tracks and horrible synth-bass sounds. The album failed both as an attempt to place Young squarely in the mainstream of then-contemporary rock, and as an album in its own right.*

Weight Of The World
A mid-'80s extravaganza, packed with cavernous drums and sampled breathing, submerges a powerful song in sterile surroundings.
Violent Side
Somewhere beneath the synthesizers and vocals from the San Francisco Boys' Choir is a troubled, paranoid Neil Young song in search of a decent arrangement.
Hippie Dream
An angry attack on David Crosby's freebase cocaine addiction, with a particularly savage guitar solo lost somewhere in the mix. Another wasted opportunity.
Bad News Beat
What would be at least a passable rocker in the hands of Crazy Horse sounds hollow and characterless here, stymied by yet another synth-heavy arrangement.
Touch The Night
One more decent song, complete with guitar solo, frustratingly and predictably demolished by *Landing On Water's* AOR

production values.

People On The Street

Stadium-rock chest-beating twaddle, complete with incongruous 'funky' slap bass playing and fearfully bland backing vocals.

Hard Luck Stories

Dated '80s synth-bass and 'epic' synthesizers are not the only problem here: the actual song is hopeless too.

I Got A Problem

Thumping drums, a garage punk riff and noisy guitar solo – mixed, as inexplicably as ever, quieter than those drums – add up to the hardest moment on the album.

Pressure

What sounds like a solo made up of sampled screams is the most arresting thing about this nondescript rocker. The horrible chanted chorus is undoubtedly the worst.

Drifter

Some furious Young soloing briefly threatens to catch fire, but the duel between guitar and a grating synthesizer sound brings the album to an unimpressive close.

Neil Young & Crazy Horse
Life

Released: June 1987
Chart Position: US: 75
UK: 71
Producers: David Briggs, Neil Young, Jack Nitzsche
Engineer: Tim Mulligan
Recorded: Westwood One, Sunset Sound, Record One, California

A return to Crazy Horse, but hardly a return to form. There are good songs here, but Young still seemed perilously in love with unnecessary synthesizer embellishments and over-production. Recorded live then overdubbed in the studio, Life *attempted to recapture the glory of* Rust Never Sleeps*, but lacked that album's inspirational spark.*

Mideast Vacation

An opening burst of synthesizer leads the listener to expect the worst, but this track, with a melody vaguely recalling 'Cortez The Killer', has a certain restrained, brooding power.

Long Walk Home

A strong piano ballad, on which Crazy Horse's trademark harmonies fight for space with overwrought synthesized fanfares and sampled explosions.

Around The World

A hollow stadium rock track with a middle-eight that inexplicably reverts to bleeping *Landing On Water* territory. Some backwards guitar aside, this is unarresting stuff.

Inca Queen

'Cortez The Killer''s lyrical territory revisited on an acoustic ballad of considerable charm, with fluid guitar and sampled effects (flute and birdsong) that actually work.

Too Lonely

'Mr. Soul'/'(I Can't Get No) Satisfaction'-style riffing married to a nondescript song that reworks the faintly offensive rock cliché of the poor little rich girl.

Prisoners Of Rock 'n' Roll

Crazy Horse rediscover some of their fire, with a thrashing snarl at 'record company clowns' with the manifesto-like chorus of 'we don't wanna be good'.

Crying Eyes

A Ducks track reworked as classic Crazy Horse thunder, complete with super-distorted guitar breaks.

When Your Lonely Heart Breaks

Another strong ballad with a tortured vocal, undersold by its AOR production: all 'atmospheric' synthesizers and booming drums.

We Never Danced

The return of arranger Jack Nitzsche, who embellished Young's affecting fantasy about purgatory with echoing piano notes to considerable effect.

Neil Young
This Note's For You

Released: April 1988
Chart Position: US: 61
UK: 56
Producer: Neil Young, Niko Bolas, aka The Volume Dealers
Engineer: Tim Mulligan, Gary Long
Recorded: November 1987–January 1988 at Studio Instrument Rentals, Studio 6, Los Angeles; The Omni, Oakland, Redwood Digital, San Francisco.

Another genre experiment, but this time successful. Young as a jazz-and-soul-influenced blues artist may not sound an appealing prospect, but the maudlin, world-weary songwriting fits perfectly with The Bluenotes' understated, gentle playing, while the title track displayed that despite his recent albums, Young was still full of lyrical fire.

Ten Men Workin'
Crisp horns power The Bluenotes' anthem along in swinging fashion, while Young's guitar-playing sounds revitalised by comparison with recent leaden outings.

This Note's For You
The dynamic power of The Bluenotes' extended line-up is shown off in a brief, but explosive attack on corporate sponsorship of rock concerts.

Coupe De Ville
A gently strummed and plaintively sung tale of a rock star on the

skids, lent extra melancholy atmosphere by The Bluenotes' jazzy, after-hours playing.

Life In The City

In sharp contrast to the preceding track, Young snarls a distorted vocal about urban decay, while the brass section lets rip behind him to dramatic effect.

Twilight

Young at his most atmospheric, conjuring up the image of dusk with beautiful interplay between guitar and horns and a metronomic tick marking the passing of time.

Married Man

A pure blues/soul pastiche, complete with rhythmic brass punctuation, a brief but thrilling solo and agreeably silly lyrics about adultery (an oft-repeated lyrical subject, incidentally). Slight, but fun.

Sunny Inside

A homage to the Stax sound, paying tribute to both Wilson Pickett – the song recalls 'In The Midnight Hour' – and Jerry Lee Lewis ('You came along and shook me honey').

Can't Believe Your Lyin'

Brushed drums, a subtle bassline and marvellously subdued playing from Young lend this tale of a man ruined by love an authentically seedy air.

Hey Hey

More explosive brass and another attack on video culture ('turn off that MTV') enlivens an otherwise unremarkable blues workout.

One Thing

Crazy Horse's Ralph Molina takes over on drums, but this is another subdued outing from The Bluenotes, wrapping mournful saxophone around a failed relationship lyric.

Crosby, Stills, Nash & Young
American Dream

Released: November 1988
Chart Position: US: 16
UK: 55
Producers: Niko Bolas, David Crosby, Stephen Stills, Graham Nash, Neil Young.
Engineers: Gary Long, Tim McCollam, Brently Walton, Joe Vitale, Graham Nash.
Recorded: February–September 1988, Redwood Digital, Woodside, California.

> *While the very existence of* American Dream *proved that Young was a man of his word – he said he would re-form Crosby, Stills, Nash & Young if Crosby cleaned up – the album itself is pretty feeble, despite the obvious tension. Young's contributions are the best things here, but they're far from his best, being easy on the ear rather than substantial. The less said about the others' contributions, the better.*

American Dream
Perky synthesized pan-pipes provide the hook, but Crosby, Stills & Nash's harmonies provide the most satisfying aspect of this tale of a public figure destroyed by scandal.

Got It Made
Name Of Love
An overly relaxed guitar duel between Young and Stills is a disappointment on a song that's pleasant rather than thrilling: the album's problem in microcosm.

Don't Say Goodbye
This Old House
Overly sentimental lyrics about house repossession and a straight country arrangement ill-suited to the foursome's soaring harmonies:

well-intentioned, but a non-starter. Wholly played by Young.

Nighttime For The Generals

Shadowland

Drivin' Thunder

A nondescript writing collaboration between Stills and Young (with Stills clearly in control) offers some startling lead guitar, but, alas, little in the way of a tune.

Clear Blue Skies

That Girl

Compass

Soldiers Of Peace

Feel Your Love

Gentle acoustic balladry, a sweet melody and more fine Crosby, Stills & Nash harmonies add up to another pleasant, but unexciting track.

Night Song

Another Stills/Young collaboration, a driving, if inconsequential, rock track that boasts some strong guitar interplay from the duo.

Neil Young
Eldorado

Released: March 1989, Japan and Australasia only
Chart Position: US: —
UK: —
Producers: Neil Young, Niko Bolas
Engineer: Tim Mulligan
Recorded: November 1988, The Hit Factory, New York,

Young jokingly dubbed these tracks 'popular music'. In fact, they were the most extreme pieces of music he'd recorded since Tonight's The Night. *Energised by the tribute album* The Bridge *in much the same way was* Rust Never Sleeps *was energised by punk, Young screamed, seethed and played apocalyptic, feedback-*

strewn guitar. Only released in Japan and Australasia.
Cocaine Eyes
The dramatic sound encapsulated: grinding guitar noise, pounding bass and drums and savage lyrics, apparently aimed at Stephen Stills.
Don't Cry
Incendiary wall-of-noise grunge, which unfurls from a gentle opening to startling, feedback-drenched mayhem by its close.
Heavy Love
Young's jagged, demented guitar-playing is matched by a frenzied vocal. By the end, Young is barely able to scream out the words.
On Broadway
A reverb-soaked cover of the much-covered Mann/Weill/Lieber/Stoller classic, with a sludgy electric guitar noise and an updated lyric – 'give me that crack!' – that attempts to makes the song Young's own.
Eldorado
Spanish guitar and maracas colour this Western tale, but the gradual increase of tension to an unbearable guitar and screamed vocal cacophony is the emotional high-point.

Neil Young
Freedom

Released:	October 1989
Chart Position:	US: 35
	UK: 17
Producers:	Neil Young, Niko Bolas
Engineers:	Harry Sitam, Tim Mulligan
Recorded:	November 1988–March 1989, Redwood Digital, Woodside, California; The Hit Factory, New York; Jones Beach Music Centre, Wantaugh, Long Island.

The long-anticipated return to form, Freedom is the equal of virtually anything in Young's 1970s catalogue.

He sounded angry and assured, offering his full range of styles, from rampaging guitar soloing to gentle acoustic balladry, with a genuinely inspired set of songs to match. It's 60 minutes long, but it's an hour well spent. The ludicrous poster inside, featuring Young wearing a beret and combat trousers and with a mouth organ around his neck is worth a chuckle too.

Rockin' In The Free World
Young rails anthemically at the failings of late-'80s America, recorded live and solo in Long Island to an audibly rapturous reception.

Crime In The City (Sixty To Zero Part 1)
Young's finest song in years: almost nine minutes of slow-building anger and disillusionment set to a compelling acoustic riff and a powerful horn section.

Don't Cry

Hangin' On A Limb
A simple, effective, melodically strong ballad, with Linda Ronstadt on backing vocals. Further proof that *Freedom* is Young's best album in a decade.

Eldorado

The Ways Of Love
This '70s-vintage song recalls *Comes A Time*, with pedal steel guitar and Ronstadt's vocal much to the fore: a strong example of Young in country mode.

Someday
A keyboard-led track with curious lyrics which take in everything from Erwin Rommel to Alaskan pipelines and bizarre backing vocals that urge us to 'praise the Lord!'

On Broadway

Wrecking Ball
An allusion to the past via a lyrical quotation from 'Like A Hurricane', but this piano-led song is lush and romantic, rather than drunken and lustful.

No More

A Crazy Horse-esque rock track, but delivered with a lighter touch than Crazy Horse could muster. Bright acoustic guitars back strong lyrics about drug addiction.

Too Far Gone
Acoustic guitar, pedal steel and mandolin propel a song reminiscent in tone and quality of *American Stars 'n' Bars,* as the maudlin drunk bemoans his misfortune.

Rockin' In The Free World
An urgent, electric, studio version of the opening track. As with *Tonight's The Night* and *Rust Never Sleeps,* the repetition is designed to emphasise its central importance.

Neil Young & Crazy Horse
Ragged Glory

Released:	September 1990
Chart Position:	US: 31
	UK: 15
Producers:	David Briggs, Neil Young
Engineer:	John Hanlon
Recorded:	Redwood Barn, Woodside, California

*Recorded in a barn on Young's ranch with Young alleged-
ly singing while standing in a pile of horse manure,
Ragged Glory revisited the freewheeling chaos of
Zuma with considerable zest. Not quite as consistent as
was claimed at the time, but with extended jams like
'Love And Only Love' and the cheerily dumb anthemics
of 'F*!#in' Up' on board, Ragged Glory could hardly fail.*

Country Home
The mighty return of Crazy Horse, reworking a 1970s Young track in a blaze of chiming guitars, wayward backing vocals and feedback.

White Line

A huge lead guitar sound powers this thrashing re-recording of a track from the abandoned *Homegrown* album.

F*!#in' Up

Crazy Horse at their most basic and reductive: thuggishly simple riffing, overdriven guitars, repetitive soloing. Lyric and title match each other well.

Over And Over

Young's voice hovers around in the vague area of the tune, yet somehow his vocal difficulties add to the power of this mid-paced song, complete with fine guitar solo.

Love To Burn

Over ten minutes of Young's extended soloing married to harmony-laden choruses in the 'Cowgirl In The Sand' style. It lacks that track's power, but remains tautly thrilling.

Farmer John

The old Premiers' hit – as covered by The Squires – bashed out in authentically chaotic garage band style.

Mansion On The Hill

Young evokes Charles Manson again on one of Ragged Glory's highlights, a wry, clear-eyed look at the passing of the 1960s.

Days That Used To Be

Young admitted this track's melodic debt to Dylan's 'My Back Pages': whether this underlines the song's nostalgic lyric or merely its lack of originality is a moot point.

Love And Only Love

A second ten minutes-plus jam, with all the ingredients for a Crazy Horse epic. Young's guitar playing is superb throughout and is *Ragged Glory*'s best moment.

Mother Earth (Natural Anthem)

An ecologically-minded live recording, with a curious but effective combination of hymn-like vocals and feedback-laden, doomy guitar.

Neil Young & Crazy Horse
Arc-Weld

Released:	October 1991
Chart Position:	US: 154
	UK: 20
Producers:	Neil Young and David Briggs with Billy Talbot
Engineer:	Phil Gitomer, Dave Roberts, Brian Leskowicz
Recorded:	February–April 1991, Civic Arena, Pittsburgh; Madison Square Garden, New York City; *Arc* assembled from various other live dates throughout tour.

Crazy Horse's remarkable Smell The Horse *US tour captured for posterity. With the Gulf War raging, the band's extended, feedback-blitzed reworkings of songs (and their crawling cover of Dylan's 'Blowin' In The Wind') took on extra resonance and the passion of their performances is clearly audible on this double CD. The bonus third disc* Arc *(later available separately) is a melange of feedback and song introductions produced by Young alone and edited into one 37-minute sequence. Hardly the easiest of listening, but a reassuringly avant-garde gesture nonetheless.*

Hey Hey, My My (Into The Black)
Crime In The City
Blowin' In The Wind
Welfare Mothers
Love To Burn
Cinnamon Girl
Mansion On The Hill
F*!#in' Up
Cortez The Killer
Powderfinger

Love And Only Love
Rockin' In The Free World
Like A Hurricane
Farmer John
Tonight's The Night
Roll Another Number
Arc

Neil Young
Harvest Moon

Released: November 1992
Chart Position: US: 16
UK: 9
Producers: Neil Young, Ben Keith
Engineers: Tim Mulligan, John Nowland
Recorded: July–November 1991, Redwood Digital, California.

The clue was in the title: this was a '90s sequel to Harvest *and* Comes A Time. *It embodied their hallmarks: polished arrangements and production; a downhome, countrified lilt and backing vocals from James Taylor, Linda Ronstadt and Nicolette Larson among others. It also embodies the earlier albums' failings: sentimental lyrics and occasionally sappy melodies.*

Unknown Legend
An appealing return to the well-produced acoustic values of *Comes A Time*, complete with Ronstadt's harmony vocal on the instantly memorable chorus.
From Hank To Hendrix
Harvest Moon's theme of the passing of time evocatively explored through pop culture icons, to a lulling background of organ and pedal steel.

You And Me
A simple acoustic song, dating back to 1971, with an eerie vocal from Young bolstered by the return of Larson on the chorus.

Harvest Moon
Young's most commercial recording in years features a beguiling melody, percussion from a sweeping broom and a charming lyric about enduring love.

War Of Man
A dull arrangement of a nondescript song about animals suffering the effects of war, although the spectacular harmony vocals on the chorus are worth waiting for.

One Of These Days
Harvest Moon occasionally errs on the side of blandness, as demonstrated by this rather cloying melody, which obscures a lyric complementing Young's various collaborators.

Such A Woman
As befits *Harvest*'s '90s cousin, a ludicrously overblown Jack Nitzsche orchestration crushes a slight but enjoyable song.

Old King
An agreeably daffy, banjo-led tribute to Young's deceased pet dog Elvis, which serves to lighten the tone of a ponderous and occasionally grim-faced album.

Dreamin' Man
A disturbing lyric – The Loner recast as homicidal gunman – softly sung and set against a beautifully played musical backdrop for maximum spooky effect.

Natural Beauty
A recording of the dawn chorus from the Brazilian rainforest provides a suitable coda to this 10-minute live track, a strong assessment of green issues.

Neil Young
Lucky Thirteen

Released: January 1993
Chart Position: US: —
UK: 69
Producer: various
Engineer: various
Recorded: 1982–1988

Compilation of the dismal years. Included some rare and previously unreleased material to shore up the dross.

Sample And Hold
Transformer Man
Depression Blues

An outtake from the cancelled Farm Aid EP, this is a straightforward country track, as unremarkable as most of Young's mid-'80s down-home experiments.

Get Gone

A live Shocking Pinks track with a dragging Bo Diddley 'hambone' beat, purporting to tell the story of Young's mythic rock 'n' roll combo.

Don't Take Your Love Away From Me

Better than everything on *Everybody's Rockin'*, this lengthy live Shocking Pinks track displays an intensity and musical conviction absent from that album.

Once An Angel
Where Is The Highway Tonight?
Hippie Dream
Pressure
Around The World
Mideast Vacation
Ain't It the Truth

An old Squires song, resurrected live and stretched to seven minutes – far beyond its worth – by The Bluenotes.

This Note's For You

Neil Young
Unplugged

Released: June 1993
Chart Position: US: 23
UK: 4
Producer: David Briggs
Engineer: Tim Mulligan
Recorded: February 7, 1993, Universal Studios, Los Angeles

Young's appearance in the Unplugged (note: no 'MTV Unplugged' title for him) series is notable for the appearance of the Stills-baiting 'Stringman', a powerful, stripped-down version of 'Like A Hurricane' performed at the pump organ and a radical reworking of Trans's 'Transformer Man' into a lilting country ballad, that lets the power of the song shine through for the first time on record.

The Old Laughing Lady
Mr. Soul
World On A String
Pocahontas
Stringman
Like A Hurricane
The Needle And The Damage Done
Helpless
Harvest Moon
Transformer Man
Unknown Legend
Look Out For My Love
Long May You Run
From Hank To Hendrix

Neil Young & Crazy Horse
Sleeps With Angels

Released: September 1994
Chart Position: US: 9
UK: 2
Producers: David Briggs, Neil Young
Engineer: John Hanlon
Recorded: October 1993–January 1994, The Complex
Studios, West Los Angeles.

Young's greatest achievement of the '90s was to recast Crazy Horse's good-natured blundering into this dark, mysterious, subdued album. A greater range of instruments were utilised than ever before, Young's lyrics were suitably trance-like and vague, and in the fourteen-and-a-half minute 'Change Your Mind', he finally updated his guitar epic style for a more troubled era.

My Heart
Tack piano and marimba combine with spectral backing vocals and a childlike lead vocal from Young to create a highly effective and original opening.

Prime Of Life
An appalling snatch of flute-playing, courtesy of Young, actually adds to the eerily quiet atmosphere of this track, the guitar restrained to the point of tension.

Driveby
A hypnotic, piano-led performance topped with disturbingly violent lyrics make it as chilling as anything Young has recorded, despite the feeling that the old man wants to get down with the kids.

Sleeps With Angels
Heavily distorted, angular guitar almost swamps Young's vocals while Crazy Horse's high-pitched interjections – 'too late!' – add a macabre desperation to the song.

Western Hero
The Unknown Soldier theme explored in a considered ballad, spiced with accordion and shards of feedback.

Change Your Mind
Young's longest song and a true return to 'Cowgirl In The Sand' territory: gorgeously melodic choruses and stately, endless soloing.

Blue Eden
Rough, discordant blues that shares lyrics with 'Change Your Mind' and acts as a diseased-sounding coda to that track. Crazy Horse even get a co-writing credit.

Safeway Cart
Another hushed and disturbing moment, this time built around a pulsating bassline and an almost whispered vocal.

Train Of Love
The tune of 'Western Hero', with new lyrics – some shared with 'Blue Eden' – adds a thematic and sonic unity to the overall album.

Trans Am
Young's train hobby makes it onto record, but it sounds as sinister as everything else on *Sleeps With Angels*: spoken vocals, a quiet guitar solo and superb backing vocals.

Piece Of Crap
A one-note riff and dumb, shouted backing vocals fail to obscure the song's basic message of ecological concern.

A Dream That Can Last
More tack piano, another throbbing bassline, another disturbing, atmospheric track ends a disturbing, atmospheric album.

Neil Young
Mirror Ball

Released:	June 1995
Chart Position:	US: 5
	UK: 4
Producer:	Brendan O'Brien

Engineer: Brett Eliason, Sam Hofstedt, Nick Dida
Recorded: January–February 1995, Bad Animals, Seattle.

> *Written and recorded in four days at the studio owned by Heart's Wilson sisters, this collaboration with Pearl Jam was of variable quality. The young grungers' playing is a strong foil for Young's vocals and guitar, and it's hard to deny the powerful spontaneity of these tracks, but some of the songs sound rather rushed and underdeveloped. Hardly a major album, but enjoyable and diverting enough.*

Song X
A song addressing the abortion issue, where Young's ambiguous stance is backed by Pearl Jam's lumbering grunge-folk. It's saved by a particularly intense solo.

Act Of Love
Another song about abortion, with a thrilling guitar duel at its core and Pearl Jam's backing reflecting the lyrics: 'slowly pounding, slowly pounding…'

I'm The Ocean
Young's most chaotic studio recording since *Tonight's The Night* buries vocals and piano beneath an impenetrable wall of noise. Spontaneous and powerful, as it happens.

Big Green Country
More chaos. Young can't reach the high notes, his voice is rendered incomprehensible by echo and Pearl Jam thrash away, wildly out of tune.

Truth Be Known
As reflective as *Mirror Ball* gets: a melancholy riff, high backing vocals from Eddie Vedder and, lyrically, a cautionary tale of failed friendships is offered.

Downtown
A cheerily Neanderthal riff is matched to lyrics which recast the line 'let's go downtown' in new surroundings and gently mock the

hippie movement.

What Happened Yesterday

Just 45 seconds of high-pitched, pump-organ-backed misery, with a melody faintly reminiscent of Young's 'Alabama'.

Peace And Love

A duet with Eddie Vedder (who co-wrote the lyrics) that once again examines hippie values to a grinding backing, with a harshly strummed acoustic guitar adding to the chaos.

Throw Your Hatred Down

Mirror Ball's weakest moment. Pearl Jam's vibrant performance and an echo-laden Young solo can't lift a banal melody and impossibly confused lyric.

Scenery

A discordant state-of-the-nation address. The distorted bass booms throughout, but at almost nine minutes, the point is rather stretched.

Fallen Angel

A brief pump organ rendition of 'I'm The Ocean' with different lyrics closes the album on a downbeat note.

Neil Young
Music From And Inspired By The Motion Picture
Dead Man

Released:	February 1996
Chart Position:	US: –
	UK: –
Producers:	Neil Young, John Hanlon
Engineer:	John Hanlon
Recorded:	Mason St Studios, San Francisco; Redwood Digital, Woodside, California

One (very long) track
Young's soundtrack to the Jim Jarmusch opus about American Indians and white settlers sounds scratchy

and improvised, mixing loosely-played guitar riffs and pump organ drones with snatches of dialogue from the film. It creates a certain atmospheric presence, but the album is, at best, a tangential deviation.

Neil Young With Crazy Horse
Broken Arrow

Released: July 1996
Chart Position: US: 31
UK: 17
Producer: Neil Young
Engineer: Tim Mulligan
Recorded: Plywood Analogue, Redwood City; Old Princeton Landing, Princeton-By-the Sea, California.

A surprising disappointment after Sleeps With Angels, Broken Arrow *saw Crazy Horse returning to formless, endless jamming, and Young to the sort of haphazard album construction that had blighted* Hawks And Doves *and* American Stars 'n' Bars. *Ending the album with a muffled, badly played blues cover seemed to epitomise the lack of effort involved.*

Big Time
The first of three extended jams that open the album, built on the flimsiest of actual songs and lacking the dynamic variety of 'Down By The River' or 'Change Your Mind'.

Loose Change
Another extended guitar workout with little to recommend it beyond its melodic similarity to Creedence Clearwater Revival's 'Down On The Corner'.

Slip Away
The best of *Broken Arrow*'s long tracks, a hazy, unsettled jam with

Young's voice at its most ethereal, distant in the mix.

Changing Highways

Crazy Horse at their most clubfooted on an electrified country stomp that recalls the low points of *American Stars 'n' Bars*.

Scattered (Let's Think About Livin')

This track bears more than a passing resemblance to *Tonight's The Night*'s 'Albuquerque', with a more cheerful melody among the guitar lines.

This Town

Another insubstantial song – ironically about boredom – coated in chugging guitars. Despite the appearance of two guitar solos, it is surprisingly brief.

Music Arcade

A lo-fi acoustic recording (the creaking of Young's stool is clearly audible) which, with its close-miked vocal and nursery-rhyme quality, is a faintly disturbing album highlight.

Baby What You Want Me To Do?

A live recording of a Jimmy Reed song covered in a heavy-handed and unappealing manner. A bewildering final choice that smells of space-filler.

Neil Young & Crazy Horse
Year Of The Horse

Released:	October 1997
Chart Position:	US: 37
	UK: 36
Producer:	'Horse'
Engineer:	Tim Mulligan
Recorded:	during the 1996–1997 World Tour.

'It all sounds the same!' protests one audience member during Year Of The Horse. "It's all the same song!"

responds Young, gleefully. It's hard, however, not to feel disappointed with Year Of The Horse, *which substitutes the aural bombardment of* Arc-Weld *with rocking but unadventurous selections from Young's back catalogue rendered in the usual extended* Crazy Horse *style.*

When You Dance, I Can Really Love
Barstool Blues
When Your Lonely Heart Breaks
Mr. Soul
Pocahontas
Human Highway
Slip Away
Scattered
Dangerbird
Prisoners
Sedan Delivery

Crosby, Stills, Nash & Young
Looking Forward

Released:	November 1999
Chart Position:	US: –
	UK: –
Producers:	David Crosby, Stephen Stills, Graham Nash, Neil Young, Joe Vitale, Ben Keith, J. Stanley Johnston
Engineers:	Tim Mulligan, Bill Halverson, Paul Dieter, Robi Banerji, Joe Vitale, Stephen Stills, Stanley Johnston, Nathaniel Kunkel, John Hausmann, Robert Breen, Devel Day, Lior Goldenberg, Tony Flores, Barry Goldberg, Ed Cherney, Aaron Lepley, Jim Mitchell
Recorded:	November 1996–February 1999 at Ocean Studios, Burbank; Redwood Digital, Woodside California; Ga Ga's Room, Los Angeles; Stray Gator Sound,

Los Angeles; Conway Studio, Los Angeles

The latest reunion, and another flop. Despite the pre-release hype which misguidedly suggested a return to late 1960s form, Looking Forward *was sadly closer in spirit to* American Dream: *Young's tracks epitomising the pleasant, but hardly thrilling acoustic material he seems to reserve for collaborative albums these days. Note the surely successful attempt to go for a world record number of engineers on a single album.*

Faith In Me
Looking Forward
A simplistic melody, delicately backed by Stills and Young's acoustic guitar picking and embellished with harmonies. Nice enough, but the earth remains unshattered.
Stand And Be Counted
Heartland
Seen Enough
Slowpoke
Its rhythm recalling 'Heart Of Gold', its chorus a classic sweep of perfect harmonies, this is the highlight of an patchy album.
Dream For Him
No Tears Left
Out Of Control
Another pleasantly inconsequential track in the gentle acoustic mode, decorated tastefully with Ben Keith's trusty pedal steel.
Someday Soon
Queen Of Them All
As close as Young seems to come to writing rock tracks for Crosby, Stills, Nash & Young these days, but 'Queen Of Them All' is marred by a rather lumpy rhythm.
Sanibel

MISCELLANEOUS GUEST APPEARANCES

The Squires
The Sultan/Aurora (single)

Released: Autumn 1963
Wrote, and plays guitar on, both tracks.

The Monkees
Head

Released: 1968
Plays guitar on 'As We Go Along'.

Various Artists
Woodstock: Three Days Of Peace And Music

Released: 1970
Includes Crosby, Stills, Nash & Young's Suite: 'Judy Blue Eyes', 'Marrakesh Express', '4+20', 'Sea Of Madness'.

David Crosby
If I Could Only Remember My Name

Released: 1971
Plays guitar and co-writes 'What Are Their Names'. Sings, plays guitar and co-writes 'Music Is Love'.

Graham Nash
Songs For Beginners

Released: 1971
Plays piano on 'I Used To Be A King'.

Grin
Grin

Released: 1971
> Young and Crazy Horse contribute to 'See What Love Can Do', 'Outlaw' and 'Pioneer Mary'. Grin were fronted by Nils Lofgren.

Buffy Sainte-Marie
She Used To Wanna Be A Ballerina

Released: 1971
> Sings and plays guitar on his own 'Helpless'.

Neil Young & Graham Nash
War Song/The Needle And The Damage Done (single)

Released: June 1972
> Wrote and co-performed the anti-Vietnam A-side in support of George McGovern's disastrous presidential campaign. B-side his own anyway.

The Band
The Last Waltz

Released: 1976
> Sings and plays guitar on his own 'Helpless'.

Joni Mitchell
Hejira

Released: 1976
> Plays harmonica on 'Furry Sings The Blues'.

Crazy Horse
Crazy Moon

Released: 1978

Plays guitar on 'She's Hot', 'Going Down Again', 'Thunder And Lightning', 'New Orleans' and 'Downhill'.

Various Artists
Where the Buffalo Roam, OST

Released: 1980

Plays guitar and sings on 'Home, Home On The Range'.

Various Artists
We Are The World

Released: 1985

Sings on Northern Lights' 'Tears Are Not Enough'.

Willie Nelson
Half Nelson

Released: 1985

Sings on his own 'Are There Any More Real Cowboys?'.

Tracy Chapman
Crossroads

Released: 1987

Plays acoustic guitar and piano on 'All That You Have Is Your Soul'.

Warren Zevon
Sentimental Hygiene

Released: 1987
Plays guitar on 'Sentimental Hygiene'.

Warren Zevon
Transverse City

Released: 1989
Sings on 'Splendid Isolation' and plays guitar on 'Gridlock'.

Emmylou Harris
Duets

Released: 1990
Wrote, sings and plays guitar on 'Star Of Bethlehem'.

Robbie Robertson
Storyville

Released: 1991
Sings on 'Soap Box Preacher'.

Nils Lofgren
Crooked Line

Released: 1992
Sings on 'Someday', sings and plays harmonica on 'You'. Plays guitars on 'Drunken Driver'.

Rusty Kershaw
Now And Then

Released: 1992

Plays harmonica and sings on 'New Orleans Rag', 'Boys In The Band', 'I Like To Live On The Bayou', 'Married Man', 'In the Backroom', 'Goin' Down To Louisiana', 'Future Song'.

Randy Bachman
Any Road

Released: 1993

Plays guitar and sings on 'Prairie Town'.

Various Artists
Bob Dylan: The 30th Anniversary Concert
Celebrations

Released:

Sang and played (with Booker T & The MGs) on 'Just Like Tom Thumb's Blues' and 'All Along The Watchtower'. Backing vocals and guitar on 'My Back Pages' and Knockin' On Heaven's Door'.

Rob Wasserman
Trios

Released: 1994

Sings and plays guitar on 'Easy Answers'.

Bobby Charles
Wish You Were Here

Released: 1994
Plays guitar on 'I Want To Be The One', 'I Remember When', 'Ambushin' Bastard' and 'I Don't See Me'.

Ben Keith And Friends
Seven Gates

Released: 1994
Co-producer. Plays pump organ on 'Silver Bells', 'The Little Drummer Boy', 'Les Trios Cloches', 'Away In A Manger' and 'Greensleeves'; guitar and vocals on 'The Little Drummer Boy' and 'Greensleeves'.

Various Artists
Philadelphia: Music From The Motion Picture

Released: 1994
Includes Young's 'Philadelphia', plus The Indigo Girls covering Danny Whitten's 'I Don't Want To Talk About It'.

TRIBUTE ALBUMS

The Bridge

Released: July 1989
Soul Asylum: Barstool Blues/Victoria Williams & The Williams Brothers: Don't Let It Bring You Down/Flaming Lips: After The Gold Rush/Nikki Sudden & The French Revolution: Captain Kennedy/Loop: Cinnamon Girl/Nick Cave: Helpless/Bongwater: Mr. Soul/Pixies:

Winterlong/Sonic Youth: Computer Age/Psychic TV:
Only Love Can Break Your Heart/Dinosaur Jr: Lotta
Love/Henry Kaiser: The Needle And The Damage
Done/Tonight's The Night (medley)/B.A.L.L.: Out Of
the Blue/Henry Kaiser: Words

The first and best of the Young tribute albums, The
Bridge *pooled together an intelligently selected collection of contemporary British and American indie bands,
with occasionally sparkling results. Pixies' 'Winterlong',
Nick Cave's rumbling version of 'Helpless' and Sonic
Youth's radical deconstruction of 'Computer Age' are par-
ticular highlights. Some of the proceeds went to The
Bridge School charity and the project was dedicated to
'physically challenged children everywhere'.*

This Note's For You Too!

Released: 1998

*Minor American alt.rock denizens cover Young on a dou-
ble compilation album. All proceeds went to Young's
Bridge charity, although he refused the compilers per-
mission to say so on the sleeve.*

Pickin' On Neil Young

Released: 1998

Country and bluegrass covers.

THREE

THE LEGACY

Thirty-four years after joining Buffalo Springfield, Neil Young remains an anomalous combination of longevity and continued influence. Lou Reed may have shifted rock music's boundaries more dramatically towards the avant-garde, but his reputation rests disproportionately on the first few albums he made with The Velvet Underground and today he remains too arty, austere and weird for mass consumption. Bob Dylan may have been considered of greater musical and intellectual import in his mid-1960s heyday, but his genius has flowered only intermittently in the last 30 years: no youth movement of the 1990s based its music and, rather wisely, its appearance on Dylan.

By contrast, Young can boast an American audience that transcends boundaries of age, fashion, politics and class. Attending a Young gig in 1993, *Rolling Stone*'s Alan Wright found men in suits and ties 'seated next to kids in frayed flannel shirts, next to preppie types in Docksiders, next to rockers in leather jackets. Garth Brooks listeners mingle with Nirvana-heads. Woodstock meets Lolapalooza.' To those who listen to balding Garth Brooks, the still-hirsute Young is the keeper of the flame, melding various traditional strands of musical Americana into his own style, while embodying half-remembered 1960s values.

To the Nirvana-heads, Young is the archetype of the tortured, frazzled songwriter, his confessional songs and open dislike of the music industry's corporate machinations spiked with angst-ridden feedback. To perennially hip, arty New York groups such as Sonic Youth, Young is a great avant-garde artist who just happens to perform in arena venues.

It's possible to find evidence to support all these theories in Young's back catalogue. It is not an overstatement to suggest that virtually every American band to emerge under the banner of alt.rock over the last 15 years has owed some kind of stylistic debt to Neil Young. From grunge to nu-country to stoner rock to lo-fi, all the multifarious and bewildering sub-genres of alternative American music seem to have been partially informed by at least one stage of Young's hugely varied career.

One reason for Young's longevity and wide-ranging influence is his sheer unpredictability. He spent the late 1960s quitting and rejoining Buffalo Springfield, stymying their career seemingly on the strangest of whims, and leaving them filed under 'unfulfilled potential'. Despite Young's continual – probably guilt-fuelled – protestations that Buffalo Springfield were among the greatest bands of the 1960s, the records they left behind are confused and distinctly underwhelming by comparison to say, The Byrds' records over the same period.

In the 1970s, he deliberately disrupted his own smooth path to superstardom by releasing *Time Fades Away* and *Tonight's The Night*. Crackling, scabrous, off-key and faintly deranged, these albums told the keen-eared fan a great deal about how Young himself felt, but were so sonically extreme as to (at least temporarily) alienate the mainstream audience that had found Young through his connections with Crosby, Stills & Nash or the gently stoned waft of *Harvest*.

In the 1980s, in the face of his running battles with record companies and changes in the musical climate he could not fully comprehend, his cussedness reached farcical levels. Young produced a string of albums in a bewildering variety of genres, most of them utterly devoid of the inspiration which had previously informed his work, yet by the 1990s the musical climate had swung so far in Young's favour that Rolling Stone magazine could unambiguously pronounce him 'the king of rock and roll'.

On the surface, his career appeared to have settled down into a cycle of vibrant excursions into distorted rock, followed by more contemplative acoustic albums, but Young was still capable of throwing artistic curveballs like *Arc-Weld*, an album constructed entirely from feedback, or the subdued menace of *Sleeps With Angels*.

'There's little that's reassuring about the Horse sound that Young, Billy Talbot, Poncho Sampedro and Ralph Molina have created here. The scouring attack that they've been perfecting since 1969's *Everybody Knows This Is Nowhere* is hovering in the background, but it's been displaced by odd instrumentation, minimalist settings and ambient atmospheres,' enthused Britain's *New Musical Express* over *Sleeps With Angels*, while Paul Williams in *Crawdaddy!* noted of the same record that 'the Neil fans I've met who don't yet appreciate *Sleeps With Angels* seem to be having trouble with their expectations of what a Neil Young & Crazy Horse album ought to sound like.'

Not even the most seasoned and well-versed fan can ever predict with total certainty what Young will do next, something of a rarity among rock stars in their mid-50s. Moreover, unlike most of his middle-aged peers, Young has never seemed particularly aligned to a specific era in music. Indeed, throughout his career Young has been more concerned with iconoclasm than celebration. He did not especially enjoy Buffalo Springfield's brief moment of celebrity: Young's Buffalo Springfield songs, such as 'Mr. Soul', 'Burned' and 'Broken Arrow' complained heartily about the vacuity and falseness of the Los Angeles music scene, just as bandmates Stephen Stills and Richie Furay celebrated its very existence in, for example, 'Rock 'n' Roll Woman' or 'Good Time Boy'.

In contrast to most of his 1960s West Coast contemporaries, Young never truly fell for the hippie dream, spotting its flaws and admitting its failings long before punk bands began sneering at its excesses. As with his idol, Roy Orbison, Young's music seemed at times to be informed by the personal tragedies of his life: for him, the idealism of the late 1960s was destroyed by the heroin-fuelled deaths of Crazy Horse guitarist Danny Whitten and Crosby, Stills, Nash & Young roadie Bruce Berry.

In 1973, *Time Fades Away*'s closing track, an endless slab of rancorous cacophony called 'Last Dance', offered a desecration of hippie philosophy as furious and negative as anything produced by Richard Hell or the Sex Pistols. 'You can live your own life, make it on your own time, laid-back and laughing,' howled Young, as his band collapsed around him. 'Oh no! Oh no! No, no, no...' At the song's close, he sang the word 'no' 67 times in a row. In a final irony, so did backing vocalists David Crosby and Graham Nash, the half of Crosby, Stills, Nash & Young who truly overdosed on the counterculture's flowery mulch.

The next year, Young followed that up with *On The Beach*, an album which made blackly comic capital out of Charles Manson's exploits on 'Revolution Blues' and offered a stark closing message on 'Ambulance Blues': 'You're all just pissing in the wind, you don't know it, but you are'.

Then came *Tonight's The Night*, on which drugs are presented as a useful means of obliteration rather than enlightenment – 'I'll roll another number for the road, I feel able to get under any load' – and Woodstock is roundly sniggered at. *Tonight's The Night*'s vision was so dark, its music so raw and unremitting, that it is far easier to draw comparisons with contemporary proto-punk bands like Pere Ubu or even Lou Reed's confrontational, audience-baiting album of white noise, 1975's *Metal Machine Music*, than it is with The Doobie Brothers or The Eagles.

Today, mocking 1960s excess is correct common cultural practice, but in the early 1970s, it was utterly out of step with prevalent trends. Most bands who chose to do so were simply ignored by critics and public alike (see The Stooges or Jonathan Richman & The Modern Lovers), but Young was a major artist with an unpalatable message. The immediate result was opprobrium – *Rolling Stone* found *Time Fades Away* 'ugly', 'silly', 'self-righteous', 'foolish' and 'arrogant', and, in Britain, the *New Musical Express* called *On The Beach* 'depressing because Neil Young isn't writing as well as he used to'. Even David Crosby, no stranger to the dark side himself, openly mocked Young for playing 'dark shit numbers' during Crosby, Stills, Nash & Young's 1974 tour.

However, with the benefit of hindsight, Young's sentiments seem prescient, accurate and inspirational. They presented a particularly potent package when coupled with his oft-expressed disdain for both the machinations of the music industry and the artistic and personal excesses which surrounded the supergroup phenomenon. He seemed abundantly aware of the gulf between Crosby, Stills & Nash's weighty moralising and the luxurious, moneyed lifestyle they led.

While David Crosby contributed the appallingly self-obsessed 'Almost Cut My Hair' and Graham Nash the well-intentioned but preachy 'Teach Your Children' to the quartet's *Déjà Vu*, Young produced 'Helpless', a simple, nostalgic celebration, offering what the lyrics called 'dream comfort memory' instead of paranoia and hollow political rhetoric.

The contrast is even more marked on *4 Way Street*, where Young is charming and self-deprecating ('this is a song guaranteed to bring you down,' he chuckles. 'It's called "Don't Let It Bring You Down"') in marked contrast to Stephen Stills, who charges through a pompous, 'improvised' political 'rap' called 'America's Children' ('We're all out there, proving to Richard Nixon that America is still the home of the brave,' etc.). 'Young spoke the plain and simple truth, while Stills bored people to death with his didactic sermonising,' claimed *Rolling Stone*, assessing the pair's relative impacts in 1975.

Such actions ensured that Young escaped the critical cull of 'boring old farts' that effectively claimed Crosby, Stills & Nash's careers in the wake of punk, even in America. In June 1977, at the height of the Sex Pistols' notoriety, Johnny Rotten was invited onto London station Capital Radio's Tommy Vance Show to play his favourite records: he chose dub reggae, Captain Beefheart and Neil Young.

At the pivotal moment when punk engendered a dramatic critical revision of rock history, Young emerged firmly on the side of the new wave. On 1979's *Rust Never Sleeps*, he managed to strike a remarkable balance, offering Young's traditional musical dichotomy – acoustic balladry and high-octane Crazy Horse rock – while eagerly endorsing the Sex Pistols on 'My, My, Hey Hey (Into The Blue)' and mocking his early-'70s cohorts on 'Thrasher', a song which also showed Young's awareness that he too could become 'stuck in the sun like dinosaurs in shrines'.

Although some established British artists had responded to punk's challenge of obsolescence (notably The Rolling Stones with their disappointing 1978 album *Black And Blue*), in America, the movement barely registered among the rock hierarchy. It would take 10 years and the rise of grunge to disseminate punk's idealism into the mainstream: as the Sonic Youth video title had it, 1989 was The Year Punk Broke in America.

For an established American artist, even one with Young's record of unpredictable statements, *Rust Never Sleeps* was a bold and adventurous move. 'Neil Young has made a record that defines the territory. Defines it, expands it, explodes it. Burns it to the ground,' proclaimed Paul Nelson breathlessly in *Rolling Stone*. '*Rust Never Sleeps* tells me more about my life, my country and rock 'n' roll than any music I've heard in years, like a new-found friend or lover pledging honesty and eager to share whatever might be important.'

Such a dramatic gesture would not reap career-saving benefits until a decade after its release, but it did ensure critical goodwill to the weaker Young albums that immediately followed. The messy, thrown-together *Hawks And Doves* was, according to *Rolling Stone*'s review, 'an instant classic built on the barest materials'. The same magazine saw the equally uninspired *Re-Ac-Tor* as 'carefully crafted studio raunch' and *Trans* as 'an intentional clash of styles', rather than a confused compromise between synthesizer experiments and more straightforward, guitar-based fare.

If Young's cynicism enabled him to transcend the era in which his success flowered, his attitude to playing and recording had – and continue to have – an equal role to play. In 1968, note-perfect virtuosity was increasingly considered rock's *raison d'être*. While Stephen Stills and similarly-minded pals Mike Bloomfield and Al Kooper could show off their skills jamming tediously through extended Bob Dylan and Donovan cover versions, entitle the resulting album *Super Session,* and receive critical plaudits for their mind-numbing arrogance, Young was about to choose Crazy Horse as a suitable backing band.

By the standards of the time, they could barely play – again, David Crosby was loudly critical of their musical abilities throughout the 1970s – but they provided the perfect foil for Young's guitar-playing. Young and Crazy Horse both prized immediacy and impact over virtuosity. Young was never a guitar hero in the flashy mode of Led Zeppelin's Jimmy Page, but he could communicate a sense of desperation, angst and feeling by unlikely techniques, thus at one memorable point on 'Down By The River', Young hits the same note 38 times in a row.

Tellingly, Lou Reed, himself hardly the model of guitar-playing orthodoxy, was among Young's fans, proclaiming the soloing on 1975's 'Danger Bird' 'the best I've ever heard'.

Perhaps because Crazy Horse were so far removed from the mainstream concept of what constituted a 'good' band in 1969, their first album with Young, *Everybody Knows This Is Nowhere*, was greeted with a mixed critical response. On release, *Rolling Stone* found it 'disappointing' by comparison with Young's self-titled overdubbed, orchestra-heavy debut: 'it falls short of his previous effort, nothing on this album touches the aching beauty of "If I Could Have Her Tonight" and "I've Loved Her So Long" or the quiet terror of "The Old Laughing Lady". His guitar work also suffers by comparison; the lyricism of the first album can only be found in faint traces here'.

Despite such sniffiness, the album remains, along with his second Crazy Horse collaboration, 1975's *Zuma*, Young's most musically influential. Both albums offered open tunings, angsty, stammering guitar solos and an aura of world-weary, stoned swampiness. Their sound is essentially that of a rough-hewn garage band, but this isn't simple good-time rock 'n' roll. Both *Zuma* and *Everybody Knows This Is Nowhere* are lent a greater emotional complexity by the ferocity of the playing and Young's tremulous voice left high in the mix. Echoes of Crazy Horse's sound can be heard in 1980s and '90s bands such as Green On Red, Dinosaur Jr. (J. Mascis's vocals were a dead ringer for Young's), Teenage Fanclub, Pearl Jam and Flaming Lips.

It's also the style to which Young would return most frequently. His 1990s renaissance was built on the *Ragged Glory* and *Freedom* albums, which essentially recast *Everybody Knows This Is Nowhere* in a more grizzled, middle-aged light.

Its swift recording techniques and endearing flaws – the vocals on 'Round and Round (It Won't Be Long)' fade in and out because Danny Whitten rocked back and forth as he sang – were mirrored throughout Young's career. With a handful of exceptions, he records with the minimum of overdubs and frequently releases albums complete with bum notes, wobbly harmonies, and Young's cracked voice straining (and often failing) to reach the high notes. The effect of such a slapdash approach has occasionally been ruinous – as British music paper *Melody Maker* pointed out, 1981's *Re-Ac-Tor* sounded as though it had been 'released to plug gaps in the calendar' – but more frequently Young's eccentric ways have produced his most satisfying albums.

Indeed, Young's music usually suffers when it's polished and perfected, as Jim McDonough noted when considering Young's most over-produced album, 1985's *Old Ways*: 'the longer

Young tinkers with something the worse it gets, and the two years Geffen sat on *Old Ways* gave Young the opportunity to create a patronising hillbilly cartoon.'

Music that was rough, raw and immediate, albums that mocked the Woodstock generation's naiveté, a surly distrust of the music industry: Young proved it was possible to embody virtually every attitude connected with punk without actually sounding like The Ramones or dressing like Richard Hell. He may have found few similarly-minded artists during the 1970s, but by the late 1980s it became apparent that Young's career had set a blueprint for loud, languidly strummed guitars and a snotty anti-corporate attitude that many other bands were willing to follow.

Despite being conceived and recorded in 1988, after Young's leanest years of critically vilified and commercially unsuccessful albums, there was no shortage of American indie bands willing to pay homage on *The Bridge*, the first (and most important) of three Young tribute albums.

In the 1990s, he was never short of alternative bands willing to support him, despite the often hostile reactions they received from the more conservative elements within Young's audience. Indeed, Sonic Youth were forced to abandon their set at the 1991 Bridge benefit concert after one song amid a hail of booing and abuse.

Inducting Young into the Rock 'n' Roll Hall Of Fame in 1995, Pearl Jam's lead vocalist Eddie Vedder announced, 'I don't know if there's been another artist that has been inducted into the Rock 'n' Roll Hall Of Fame to commemorate a career that is still as vital as his is today.'

Since Buffalo Springfield's uncomfortable brush with teen stardom – albeit virtually confined to the Los Angeles area – Young has spent the rest of his career debunking the myth of the rock star as glamorous and all-powerful, an idea with clear appeal to the self-loathing, failure-obsessed grunge movement of the 1990s. Other than his brief mid-'60s flirtation with a Hollywood Indian image, Young has never, ever looked glamorous. In the 1970s, he resembled a particularly dressed-down member of the audience who had somehow wandered onstage by mistake, and on the 1973 *Tonight's The Night* tour, he frankly looked more like a druggy vagrant than anything.

In the 1980s and '90s, his look became even weirder. One '90s interviewer was startled to find Young wearing a coat 'so unsettling to the eye it looked as though he had won it off some ill-attired Red Indian wino during a friendly card game.' On the 1978 *Rust Never Sleeps* tour (and again in 1987 and 1991), he performed on stage sets which dwarfed both him and his band, and he gave his roadies bizarre costumes. Everything seemed designed to diminish the star of the show himself. His voice has always sounded frail, plaintive and otherworldly, while his songs have consistently revelled in failure rather than in celebrating success: 'Mr. Soul', 'The Loner', 'Tired Eyes' ('he tried to do his best, but he could not'), 'Prisoners Of Rock 'n' Roll' ('we don't wanna be good'), 'F*!#in' Up', 'Piece Of Crap'. The sentiments of those songs, as well as their sound, were markedly similar to those of Kurt Cobain, Nirvana's leader. Cobain's songs depicted human frailty in intense terms, his group's debut British tour was dubbed Lamefest, and even the T-shirts produced by leading Seattle grunge label Sub Pop, Nirvana's original home, bore the legend LOSER.

Indeed, so much cutting-edge rock music was produced in Neil Young's image by bands in the 1990s that albums which essentially revisited old territory were greeted and reviewed as if they were a major development in popular music. *Ragged Glory* was a strong Crazy Horse effort that nevertheless broke little new ground. However, surrounded by similarly-minded grunge acts 20 years younger than the members of Crazy Horse, it was heralded by British magazine *Select* as 'a stone classic...immaculate'. Young's decidedly mixed collaboration with Pearl Jam, *Mirror*

Ball, was pronounced 'the best album Pearl Jam have been involved with to date', although that, of course, may well be true.

The remarkable *Sleeps With Angels* and the overwhelming *Arc-Weld* aside, Young spent most of the 1990s indulging in what the critic Paul Williams described as 'an experiment to see what happens when you sample yourself, when you bring your famous old sounds and melodies back together for a 20-year reunion'. There was nothing fundamentally wrong with Young's 1990s albums, but little to rival the dramatic influence his 1970s recordings had exerted. Nevertheless, even Young's most disappointing work – the albums he made in the mid-1980s – became subject to critical revisionism.

The 1980s seemed to be the one musical era that Young was utterly bewildered by. While all around him moved to ever-slicker production and marketing techniques, Young, whose aversion to both slick production and marketing was almost legendary, appeared to go completely mad. He alternately attempted to embrace the zeitgeist or deny its very existence. *Trans* was a failed attempt to marry Young's songwriting with then-current technology. The two albums that followed journeyed into the past, seemingly trying to ignore what was happening around them by offering first rockabilly (*Everybody's Rockin'*), then saccharine, overcooked Nashville country (*Old Ways*). *Landing On Water* and *Life* returned to the original plan, but Young's songs and Crazy Horse's playing were ill-suited to the sterile, synthetic production.

After grunge began to emerge, and Young returned to form with the traditionally rocking *Freedom* in 1989, this era was frequently cast not as a desperate failure, but as an example of Young's mercurial talent and indomitable spirit. Thus, the argument ran, he did not make bad records because he was directionless and confused, he made them to defy his record company, who were attempting to influence his artistic direction.

'I gave *Everybody's Rockin'* a four-star review when it was released and I still don't begrudge Young a single one of them,' wrote American critic David Fricke in British magazine *Mojo*, a decade after the album's release. 'I don't play the album much any more – OK, hardly at all – but I believe that in rock 'n' roll, attitude is at least seven-tenths of the law.'

It's a nice idea – underlined by the understandably selective 1994 compilation *Lucky Thirteen*, on which Young cherry-picked the few good moments from his mid-1980s catalogue and added a few unreleased selections to cast everything in a far better light – but the fact remains that, on listening to *Everybody's Rockin'* or *Old Ways*, it becomes immediately apparent why label boss David Geffen was so vehemently opposed to their release. Young was so ill-suited to the styles he attempted that the finished results sound more karaoke than celebration.

The path of rock history in the 1990s makes it easy to view Young as a crusader for extreme music, continually confounding expectation and at odds with his audience. Even so, he has also hedged his bets, running an intermittent alternative career as a crowd-pleaser. His greatest commercial success has always been achieved with albums unafraid to conform to the common public perception of Young as the melancholy, country-influenced folkie introduced by 1970's *After The Gold Rush*. With predominantly acoustic, harmony-laden songs such as 'Birds', 'Tell Me Why' and 'Only Love Can Break Your Heart', this album established Young in a context the general public could understand, albeit rather reductively, as the latest in a line of troubled singer-songwriters, headed by James Taylor.

The critical reaction was close to hysterical. In England, *Melody Maker* writers voted it album of the year – NEIL YOUNG GOLDRUSH IS ON! screamed the headline – and Young's first major solo commercial success followed. But *After The Gold Rush* adopted the same recording techniques as *Everybody Knows This Is Nowhere*. It was simple, unadorned, and recorded at Young's Topanga Canyon home, while subsequent attempts in the same vein tended to gild the lily. *Harvest*, which remains Young's biggest-selling album, was padded with overdubs to the point of anodyne radio-friendliness, a fate which also befell 1992's *Harvest Moon* and, to a lesser extent, 1978's *Comes A Time*.

While the starkness of *After The Gold Rush* can be seen to inform the work of 1990s lo-fi country artists such as Bonnie Prince Billy (a trend begun with Victoria Williams & The Williams Brothers' muffled rendition of 'Don't Let It Bring You Down' on the tribute album *The Bridge*), Young at his most sumptuous has achieved large sales, but generally little in the way of lasting influence.

Even Young seems aware that these albums do not necessarily represent his best or most adventurous work. *Harvest* was 'probably the finest record that I've ever made, but that's a really restricting adjective for me'; while *Comes A Time* 'sounds nice...but I'm someplace else now.'

Likewise, there is the question of his schizophrenic attitude to performing his back catalogue live. Frequently, he has roundly criticised his audience from the stage for demanding he play his old hits ('you're living in the past,' he told one early-1990s heckler, before having him removed from the auditorium), yet on other occasions, he has seemed perfectly happy to strap on an acoustic guitar and trot out 'Sugar Mountain' or take to the piano for 'After The Gold Rush'. It is a precarious balance to strike, and his attempts at crowd-pleasing have not always been successful – witness the flat Stills-Young Band's *Long May You Run*, the last two Crosby, Stills, Nash & Young albums and *Landing On Water*, his 1986 attempt at recasting his style in the 1980s stadium rock idiom – but more frequently, they have worked perfectly, maintaining or regaining an audience unimpressed by his more estoric leanings. It's little surprise that *Harvest Moon* followed his most extreme album of the 1990s, the feedback-laden live package *Arc-Weld*. Young continues, perhaps uniquely in music, to mean all things to all people.

Most artists leave a musical legacy of influence and

importance because they spearhead a new scene or musical style: Bob Dylan and The Byrds jointly claim responsibility for folk-rock, Chic for disco, while Pink Floyd and The Grateful Dead have claims to different strands of psychedelia, as do the Sex Pistols and The Clash for punk. But Neil Young has been influential precisely because he did not fully conform to any movement or scene during his career. His music is essentially as impossible to categorise or pigeonhole (Folk? Country-rock? Art-rock? Proto-grunge?) as it is to predict. For this reason, his influence covers an enormous spread of musicians currently working in differing arenas: from Pearl Jam to REM to Pavement to The Flaming Lips. But his influence extends beyond the music he produced: the attitude by which his albums were informed seems equally important when considering his impact.

Young's values are fundamental to the spirit of rock 'n' roll: that it should be raw, emotional, adventurous, untainted by commercial consideration. Even when he has fleetingly abandoned those values, he has managed smartly to justify his actions. His records have been good, bad and all points in between, but his career has never been predictable or boring. He is the epitome of an artist who has managed to sustain a lengthy career without being seen to truly compromise his integrity. Anyone who can emerge from both the decadent horror of Crosby, Stills, Nash & Young and the disastrous series of albums he produced between 1983 and 1987 with their critical reputation pretty much intact is either a visionary, a master strategist or blessed with incredible luck. With Neil Young, it's probably all three.

At its most basic, Young's musical legacy can be heard whenever anyone cranks up the distortion, strums some opentuned chords on a guitar and sings plaintively about their emotions. In the 1990s, that was an extremely regular occurrence. But on another level, Young's longevity is testament to a refusal, however stubborn and wrongheaded, to do what is expected of him.

INDEX

INDEX

Picture section page 1 top: Chuck Boyd/Redferns; bottom: Michael Ochs Archives/Redferns. 2 top: Robert Altman/Arena; bottom: Michael Ochs Archives/Redferns. 3: Michel Linssen/Redferns. 4 top: Ebet Roberts/Redferns; bottom: David Redfern/Redferns. 5 top: Ebet Roberts/Redferns; bottom: Dick Barnatt/Redferns. 6 top: Henrietta Butler/Camera Press; bottom Ebet Roberts/Redferns. 7 top: Paul Howell/Liaison Photo Agency; bottom: Evan Agostini/Liaison Photo Agency. 8: "PA" Photo Agency/EPA.